Heidelberg Castle

Heidelberg Castle,
J. W. Schirmer, 19th century

Wolfgang Wiese

Heidelberg Castle

A Guide to the Castle and Gardens

Published by the
Administration of State Palaces and Gardens
Baden-Württemberg
Karlsruhe Superior Financial Authority

UMSCHAU ∶ BRAUS

Inside front cover: construction-phase plan
Inside back cover: ground plan of the Castle complex

Picture credits:
Bayerische Staatsgemäldesammlungen München 15
Generallandesarchiv Karlsruhe 89, 90
Kreisbildstelle Heidelberg 4, 10, 25, 26, 27
Kurpfälzisches Museum Heidelberg 16, 18, 21, 22, 23, 24, 28,
29, 30, 31, 32, 33, 37, 38, 39, 40, 44, 45, Seite 2
Landesbildstelle Baden 1, 3, 5, 6, 8, 9, 12, 17, 19, 35, 36, 41,
47, 51, 52, 53, 54, 55, 56, 57, 59, 60, 61, 63, 64, 65, 66, 67,
68, 69, 70, 71, 72, 73, 74, 75, 76, 77, 78, 79, 80, 82, 83, 84,
85, 86, 87, 88, 91, 92, 93, 94, 95, 96, 97, 98, 99, 100, S. 95
Staatliche Kunstsammlungen Weimar 42
Staatliche Schlösser und Gärten Baden 7, 11, 14, 20, 34, 43,
46, 48, 49, 50, 62, 81
Stadtbibliothek Heidelberg 101, 102
Stadtmuseum Amberg 13
Universitätsbibliothek Heidelberg 58
Franz Schlechter 61, 67, 71, 77, 79, 93, 95
Foto Lossen 2

Photography:
Arnim Weischer, Steffen Hauswirth, Andrea Rachele
(Landesbildstelle Baden)
Dorothea Berlinghof (Kreisbildstelle Heidelberg)
R. Burkhardt (Stadtbibliothek Heidelberg)

English translation:
Philip Mattson

© 1999 Umschau Braus, Heidelberg
ISBN 3-8295-6324-8

Cover design: Stankowski + Duschek, Grafisches Atelier
Stuttgart
Typesetting, lithography: Text & Grafik, Heidelberg
Total production: EBS, Verona

Fig. 1
Heidelberg, city and Castle
1996

A Word on the History
of Heidelberg Castle

Heidelberg Castle, on its throne above the Neckar
Valley, is a unique example of German cultural
history. Having gained fame not only as an historic
building, but also as a motif in literature and art,
today it attracts more than a million visitors a year.
Its attraction is due to the mighty aspect of the
whole as well as the visible effects of the wounds
of history and the will to preserve its appearance.
The rise and fall of the ruling House of the Electors
Palatine, but also its glorification and turning it into a
museum are the determining factors in the history
of Heidelberg Castle.

The Old Residence of the Counts Palatine of the Rhine

Heidelberg Castle is closely linked with the founding of the city of Heidelberg. Heidelberg appears in
a document for the first time in 1196, and already in

Abb. 2
Heidelberg Castle facing the Neckar

Abb. 3
Heidelberg Castle, Hubert Sattler, um 1900, Staatliche Schlösser und Gärten Baden (SSG)

1225 a fortress with the same name ("castrum in Heidelberg cum burgo ipsius castri") is mentioned. No less a figure than Konrad of Hohenstaufen, the brother of Emperor Frederick Barbarossa, had in 1155 received the Rhine-Frankish region from the patrimony of his uncle, Herman of Stahleck and his aunt, Gertrude of Swabia, and expanded Heidelberg to a major town, presumably with a castle. The Counts Palatine of

Abb. 4
Heidelberg, the City and
Castle (detail), after Matthäus
Merian, 1620, Kurpfälzisches
Museum Heidelberg (KMH)

the Rhine, who were descendants of the
Wittelsbach dynasty, whose first major representative is Ludwig I (1214-1228), were in turn heirs of the
Hohenstaufen dynasty. A document of 1303 even
lists two fortresses in Heidelberg, one of them
higher up on Gaisberg and the lower one on
Jettenbühl. Of the upper one only archeological fin-
dings and a few sketches have been preserved,
from which hardly any picture can be deduced. The
early lower fortress, in contrast, the precursor to
the Castle of today, can be pictured in rather good
detail.

The usual scheme of a fortification complex with
keep and fortification walls was preserved down to
the present day, despite sweeping changes in the
buildings. Where the "Exploded Tower" stood was
presumably where the keep was, and the adjoining
wall to the southwest appears to have been the bulwark, including an outer moat facing the hill. At the
other points there were probably already surrounding walls. Inside these walls were presumably the
palace with a heated, hall-like building, heated apart-
ments, the chapel and servants' quarters. Perhaps
most of the buildings were still of wood and were
only gradually replaced by stone structures.

Abb. 5
The Exploded Tower and
Fortification Wall

The Family Seat of the Electors Palatine

The medieval family seat of the Palatine
Wittelsbachs probably goes back to the late 13th
century, based on the dynastic developments of the

Abb. 6
Coat-of-arms of the Electors
Palatine in the Frederick
Palace

time. After Count Palatine Rudolph I (1294–1319), the progenitor of the older Wittelsbach Line, received the Rhenish lands from his father, Ludwig II of Upper Bavaria (1253–1294), the political significance of the Count Palatine was made clear for the first time. For Rudolph was married to the daughter of the German King Adolf of Nassau (1292–1298), his brother Ludwig the Bavarian (1328–1347) had become the Holy Roman Emperor, and his son Rudolph II (1327–1353) became the first Palatinate Elector in 1329. Understandably, now that they were amongst the leading princes of the German Empire, the Electors Palatine needed a seat of power which

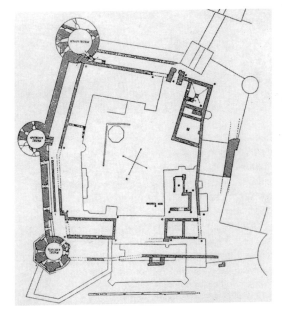

Abb. 7
Groundplan of the Castle
around 1450 (from Koch and
Seitz)

could be seen from afar rising above the town. This desire was intensified with Rupert I (1353–1390), the founder of the University and first Elector Palatine, and under Rupert III (1398–1410), Elector Palatine and German King, led to a concentrated effort on expanding the Castle. It was no longer enough to have a simple defensive fortress; now grandeur and the style of the building were of prime importance. The result was a nearly quadrangular interior courtyard with two surrounding rings of walls. Between them was a deep moat on the south, east and west sides called the "Enclosure". To the north and west the terrain dropped steeply, necessitating the construction of supportive walls. The east side was not built in a straight line, but

Abb. 8
Rupert Palace, from the east

had a slight outward bend. At the north and south corner and at the point of the bend there were fortification towers to protect the less protected east side, with its slightly dropping terrain. Walls and towers presumably had a severe purposive architectural structure.

In the interior, several buildings were constructed against the walls around the central courtyard which sloped downward to the north. The Rupert and Ludwig Palaces, Hall-of-Mirrors Building and Ladies Palace still contain parts of the original fortress. They possibly replaced wooden buildings which determined the basic groundplan. The buildings appear to have had residential and economic functions. However, one should not assume that there was any particular regulation to the way they were used, as public representation did not take place at the fortress exclusively. Whether improvements were considered under King Rupert, between 1400 and 1410, is not known. The few remains from that early building phase hardly permit conclusions to be made. It was not the fortress, but the Augustinian monastery in the town which the King chose as a temporary residence.

King Rupert

Fig. 9
King Rupert and Queen
Elizabeth, memorial slab in
the Church of the Holy Ghost,
Heidelberg

With Rupert III (1400–1410) the Electors Palatine attained the title of king for the first time and with it the highest position in the German Empire. The moment this occurred, to be sure, was very unfavourable, for the members of the Empire, which had been growing weaker for a long time, were occupied with their own territorial interests, and two Popes had brought about a schism in the Church. In 1408 there was even a third Pope. Rupert did not succeed in removing these far-reching problems. He quarreled with Wenceslaus of Bohmia (1376–1400) over the German crown and was unable to establish comprehensive power. In relations with the Church his efforts at unification were indeed a failure, but he reserved his decision for later. His success lay thus more in the territorial policies within the Palatinate, where he acquired more lands and secured the interests of his house.

The Fortress

A more sweeping expansion of the Castle complex took place at the outset of the 16th century, changing the Castle into a fortress. Under the Electors Palatine Frederick the Victorious (1451–1476) and Ludwig V (1508–1544), also called the Peaceable, a much enlarged defensive complex came about, rising imposingly above the town of Heidelberg. Heidelberg was threatened time and again, and adversaries advanced right up to the walls. These experiences caused Ludwig to move to secure it by greater fortification.

Fig. 10
Heidelberg Castle in 1543,
detail from Sebastian
Münster's "Kosmographia"

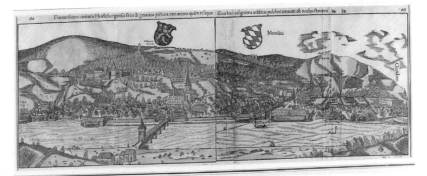

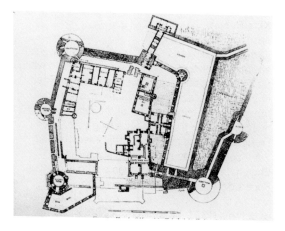

Fig. 11
Ground plan of the Castle
after 1544 (from Koch and
Seitz)

First the western side had to be expanded and
made as impregnable as possible. A broad west
front was piled up which was fortified with a high
wall. Toward the Neckar side the wall was given a
mighty tower, the "Thick Tower". The midpoint of
the west wall was the rondel, another strategic
point facing westward. Between the newly fortified
western and the south wall of the Castle a broad
and deep moat was dug, whose opening, towards
the Neckar, was closed by a passageway. A new
entrance from the hillside was secured by a large
gateway tower, a drawbridge and a house on the
bridge. Moreover, the southwest corner of the
outer castle walls was given a tower, called
"Seldom Empty" (it was presumably a prison).
The south shielding wall was considerably bolstered
and the bell tower to the northeast enlarged.
The access to the Castle from below was now not
the only one and was given an armory. Elector
Palatine Ludwig V also began building above the
inner ring of walls, as the new large moat provided
sufficient security. Thus, he built the Library
Building on the west wall between Rupert Palace
and King's Palace and Ludwig Palace to the east.
The already extant courtyard buildings were given
sturdier walls. Rupert Palace, the King's Palace and
the Soldiers Building were made more massive and
built higher.

Fig. 12
Elector Palatine Ludwig V. ,
Sebastian Götz

Ludwig V.

Ludwig V, the son of Elector Philip of the Palatinate (1476-1508), pursued an integrative policy by allying closely with the Imperial Hapsburg dynasty and reconciling differences with Wurttemberg, Hesse, Bavaria and Bohemia. He became a mediator between rival parties not as a strong personality, but as a rather timid personality who preferred avoiding conflicts. In the period of the early Reformation he was also effective as a man of compromise, even though he did not develop a deep religious faith. When Martin Luther visited Heidelberg in 1518, he guaranteed him safe conduct and the chance to hold discussions with his university professors. It was not until his feud with Francis of Sickingen that Ludwig V resorted to military means. In the Peasants' Revolt of 1525 he took a great deal of booty, which was a boon to the building of his residence.

The Castle of the Electors Palatine in the Modern Era

After the expansion of the Castle to a large defensive complex, Ludwig V's successors, the Electors Palatine Frederick II (1544–1556) and Ottheinrich (1556–1559) began with the decorative improvement of the construction. After 1544 the façades and rooms take on ornate form. Frederick II, the younger brother of Ludwig V, had spent his youth travelling in Europe and in military service, particularly at the Hapsburg Court. Here he became a proponent of Charles V, for whom he secured the vote of his brother, Ludwig V, at the imperial election of 1530. Despite his many sojourns abroad he was always in communication with the Electorate of the Palatinate. After his marriage to Dorothea of Denmark, Prince Frederick held court in Amberg Castle in the Upper Palatinate. His plans to ascend

Fig. 13
Elector Palatine Frederick II,
Bartel Behaim, 1544,
Stadtmuseum, Amberg

the Danish throne were dashed when he became the ruler of the Electorate of the Palatinate. Amongst this ruler's great problems was his lack of

Fig. 14
Hall-of-Mirrors Building, photograph, c. 1904

descendants, for Bavaria was again laying claim to the Electoral title. But at the behest of the Emperor the hereditary succession of Frederick's nephews from the House of Neuburg were declared valid. Moreover, Frederick was granted the privilege to include the imperial apple in his coat-of-arms (imperial vicariate), clearly preferential treatment of the Electorate of the Palatinate over Bavaria.

Scarcely had Frederick II taken possession of Heidelberg Castle when he began new building activity. He appears not to have been satisfied with having a fortress castle, but strived to build a residential one. Thus, representative functions were to go hand in hand with defensive ones. During his travels Frederick had become acquainted with the Renaissance, and he wanted to have this style be expressed in his Castle, too. With the Hall-of-Mirrors Building he erected a modern building in 1548–56. It was placed not toward the hill, but facing the valley; its position was thus exposed.

Fig. 15
Elector Palatine Ottheinrich, Sebald Beham, 1535, Bayerische Staatsgemälde-sammlung, Munich

Ottheinrich

The further expansion of the Castle was furthered above all by Elector Palatine Ottheinrich (1502–1559). In only a few years, the popular ruler erected monuments to himself. In the process he was more consistent in promoting modern architecture, which he had become acquainted with in Italy, Holland and Palestine. Renaissance art became his exclusive standard. At 19, Ottheinrich had become the regent of a Palatinate possession in Neuburg on Danube. Here he not only had construction done in the modern architecture of the day, but also began to collect valuable European art works, which gained him the reputation of a patron of the arts. Even today there are gobelins, paintings etc. from his art collections to be found in Bavarian museums. The Reformation also influenced this prince. In 1542 he professed his faith in the new doctrine, due to which he lost his domain of Neuburg for a time during the Schmalkaldic War of 1547 between Catholics and Protestants and was forced to flee to Heidelberg. Ottheinrich was the actual Reformer of the Electorate of the Palatinate, not his uncle, Frederick II. When the latter died in 1556 with no heirs, Ottheinrich came to Heidelberg with all his art treasures. But the Castle had no suitable place to keep all these priceless items. For this reason he had a representative domicile built for his art treasures. Not the existing buildings, which were either fortress-like or medieval in appearance, but a modern Renaissance palace was to bear witness to his claim to power over the burgeoning land.

Fig. 16
Ottheinrich Palace, west façade, Johann Ulrich Kraus, c. 1683, KMH

The Renaissance Palace

On the northeast side of the Castle courtyard, between the Hall-of-Mirrors Building and Ludwig Palace, Ottheinrich Palace with its four storeys was built, which is in ruins today. It spanned the inner enclosure moat and wall, just as the Library Building had done since the days of Ludwig V. But the new building was given a representative outer façade facing the courtyard. A double outdoor stairway leads up to the first storey. In the middle of the front the entry portal was placed, crowned by the coat-of-arms and Ottheinrich's bust. Cornices separated the storeys above it from one another, but they were visibly bonded by semipillars and pilasters. The four or five window axes of each storey were arranged in strict symmetry. An intricate decorative arrangement was distributed over the façade. Figures from the Old Testament and the gods of antiquity were placed in niches between the windows and the grotesque decorations on the architraves, pilasters and window gables. The arrangement of the relief ornaments and stone sculptures was not arbitrary, but were rather part of a classical system of arrangement devised by the Roman architect Vitruvius. Above pillars with Ionic capitals were Corinthian pilasters and Corinthian semipillars. However, a strict sequence was not adhered to. Thus, Doric and Ionic elements occur in combination. Old pictures show Ottheinrich Palace crowned by only two oddly striking dormers. It is not known if they were originally connected by a

Fig. 17
Coat-of-arms tablet above the portal of Ottheinrich Palace, c. 1558

16

saddleback roof. At the death of Ottheinrich in 1559, the building appears not to have been completed. That can be surmised from the short reign of this Elector.

The question as to who created Ottheinrich Palace has been brought up again and again. Closely linked to it is also the identification of the style and forms used. With the Dutch sculptor Alexander Colin, of Mechelen, a contract was concluded on March 7, 1558 for the pillars in various rooms, for the portal and the fireplaces and, later, for statues and window posts. A sculptor named Antoni is also mentioned. That these artists also provided the design of the entire building or at least of the façade, cannot readily be concluded. For this reason, recent scholarly literature believes an architect to be the designer of the building. Certainly the basic Italian character of the Palace is beyond doubt, which a German or Dutch master could have designed while closely adhering to Italian forms. Without a doubt Ottheinrich Palace can be called "the noblest blossoming of the German early Renaissance".

The Calvinists

With the death of Ottheinrich the rule of the old line of Electors in the Palatinate came to an end. Then followed Frederick III (1559-1576) from the House of Palatinate-Simmern. The ruler, under the influences of his counsellors, turned to the Calvinist doctrine. Only during a short transitional phase did Philip Melanchton have a major say. With the "Heidelberg Catechism" Calvinism made its breakthrough, whereas it held little sway in the rest of Germany. As he was more preoccupied with religious questions, Frederick III was little inclined to make any changes in the Castle. But this changed with John Casimir, the administrator of the Palatinate from 1583 to 1592, and with Elector Palatine Frederick IV (1583-1610). Both were instrumental in restoring Calvinism after the rule of Ludwig VI (1576-1583), who had leaned toward Lutheranism. The doctrine was definitively established, and now there was again time to occupy oneself with improvements to the residence.

Fig. 18
John Casimir of the Palatinate, engraving by Wolfgang Kilian, KMH

Under John Casimir the Castle was expanded by the Barrel Building, which was placed in front of the Ladies Building. This interrupted the northern outer ward, to be sure, weakening the line of defense, but a large battery aimed at the valley made up for it. The positioning of the building was new, as it broke out of the garland of buildings around the courtyard completely and protrudes toward the town.

Fig. 19
Elector Palatine Frederick IV,
Sebastian Götz, c. 1605

A Monument for the Ancestors

With Frederick IV the orientation toward the town was continued. This Elector had a sumptuous palace built between the Hall-of-Mirrors Building and the Ladies Building, called Frederick Palace. There was a façade toward the valley as well as one on the courtyard side, both richly decorated with sculpture. A classical arrangement of pillars and pilasters as well as cornices in the Renaissance style give the building a clearly proportioned structure of the storeys. But in its juxtaposition to the Ottheinrich Palace it is powerful and dynamic. Massive architectural elements are in a rhythmic dialogue with supportive and filling constructive elements. The structural elements in the mode of the ancients in accordance with Vitruvius' scheme are more clearly adopted than in the Ottheinrich Palace. The Tuscan order follows on the Doric, then comes the Ionic, and finally, on the dormers, the Corinthian. The gables and window decorations also follow this scheme. Only in regard to the figural decoration do the façades of the building differ. Thus, on the courtyard side, there is a stronger emphasis in that Frederick IV had a sculptural gallery of ancestors put there to place his house in the ranks of the most significant European dynasties.

The selection and placement of the figures appears less felicitious in part. But the sculptural execution and the architectural arrangement are remarkable. Two artists who gave the building their stamp should be named: the architect Johannes Schoch from Strasbourg (c. 1550-1631) and the sculptor Sebastian Götz from Chur (documented from 1604-1621). They worked in accordance with the architectural theories of mannerism. Schoch's architectural views can for this reason not be overestimated for the development of German architecture around 1600. He seems to have derived his basic architectural ideas from Ottheinrich Palace. In doing so, he formed a unique work of art which unites classical clarity (the pillar arrangement) and manneristic playfulness (grotesque decorations). In Frederick Palace Schoch drew on plentiful stores of styles and formed a magnificent façade of harmoniously arranged elements and great unity.

Fig. 20
Frederick Castle, photograph,
c. 1904, SSG

The Winter King

Frederick IV's penchant for stately representation was carried on by his son and successor, Frederick V (1610–1632). As a youthful ruler, his was an illustrious career of only a few years. In his zest for action, Frederick V placed himself at the head of the Protestant Union and became involved in politics on a European scale. First, his marriage in 1613 to

Fig. 21
Elector Palatine Frederick V, Gerrit van Honthorst, c. 1620, KMH, loan from the Baden-Wurttemberg Ministery for Science and Art (MWK)

Elizabeth Stuart, the daughter of the English King James I (1603–1625), was intended to procure recognition and security. Then, in 1619, he accepted the election as King of Bohemia, although relatives and friends had advised him not to for political reasons. The Hapsburg dynasty felt that Frederick had become too powerful, and so by 1620 Emperor Ferdinand II (1619–1637) marched his armies against him. He defeated the young king in the Battle of the White Mountain, near Prague. His rule lasted but one year (Oct. 1619 – Oct. 1620), so that he was given the name "The Winter King". The Thirty Years War (1618-1648) had broken out by this time, and as a consequence Frederick also lost his ancestral lands and the leadership of the Protestant Union in 1623. This was a painful loss, from which the Electoral Palatinate, until then one of the major powers in the German Empire, was hard put to recover. The war also came to Heidelberg, and Frederick V had to flee into exile. He fled to Holland, where found a new home in Rhenen. In 1633 he died, after repeated attempts to return via Mainz. Not only were his lofty titles gone forever, but also the unification of the two Wittelsbach dynastic branches, and thus the possibility of a leading position in Europe was again far off.

The Last Residential Building

The ascent and fate of the ruler was shared by Heidelberg Castle, as well. Just a few years before the beginning of Frederick's reign, the two magnificent palaces of his predecessors had been completed. In his lust for ostentation, the Elector Palatine

began immediately with the building of a further palace, which was to become a home which would fulfill his young wife's expectations. But all the space on the plateau of the Castle was occupied, and so only a place outside the fortress ring could be found to offer space for a grand building. The

Fig. 22
English Palace, Christian Philipp Koester, c. 1831, KMH

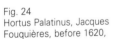

Fig. 23
Salomon de Caus, 1619,
KMH

Fig. 24
Hortus Palatinus, Jacques
Fouquières, before 1620,

north wall of Ludwig's fortress, between the Thick Tower and the Barrel Building or Ladies Building was the proper spot to create a palace of comparable dimensions to Frederick Palace. Thus, the north front of the Castle, with Frederick Palace, the Hall-of-Mirrors Building, and Bell Tower, spread above the town as a broad, powerful façade and gave the whole a unique character.

But Frederick V did not commission a repetition of the extant architectural forms, but, the adaptation of its dimensions to the existing buildings notwithstanding, provided an opportunity for a new style to be established. The building, now no longer opening on the courtyard, but completely oriented to the town below, appears in all its classical simplicity. On a high foundation the two-storey building rises, crowned by two dormers. Now it is not so much the horizontal cornice arrangements, but vertical pilasters extending over both storeys which make up the more generous appearance of the main façade opening entirely toward the town below. Ornamental or sculptural decoration are almost completely absent. In the design playful details were not the important thing, but clear proportions. The relationship of the elements to one another and the monumental effect in the proximity of the Thick Tower were important. Precisely in England around 1600 the Italian High Renaissance held sway, and

because of the new dynastic ties with the English throne, the Electoral Palatinate was also well advised to follow this example. The English architect Inigo Jones, in his enthusiam for Andrea Palladio's architecture, could have provided the plans, as Jones is known to have visited Heidelberg in 1613. But the architect of Frederick Palace, Johannes Schoch, or, more recently, the Nuremberg architect Jakob Wolff the Younger have also been suggested as the architect of the English Palace. But this unsolved mystery cannot challenge the significance of the building for the history of architecture. The English Palace may be said to be the earliest example of Palladian classicism in Germany.

A far more famous addition under Frederick V is the Hortus Palatinus. This is the large Castle Garden, built between 1616 and 1619 on the southeast terraces above Friesental. Although probably never completed, it enjoyed the reputation throughout Europe of a "miraculous garden" even while it was being built. It was regarded as the "eighth wonder of the world"., for never before had such a large artificial garden been created, with a plethora of exotic plants, ornamental flower beds, arbours, mazes, waterworks, sculptures, grottoes and pleasure houses. In the style of the Renaissance the French engineer and garden architect Salomon de Caus, summoned from England, designed the various levels of the terraces, while paying no heed to the Castle's defensive concerns. Now it would not be walls and moats, but artistic splendour and the ostentation of power which would command respect of Frederick's adversaries. But this view was too far removed from reality, for which reason the "magic garden" was not destined to endure.

Fig. 25
Hortus Palatinus, Porticus with niche, S. de Caus

Fig. 26
Fountain, S. de Caus

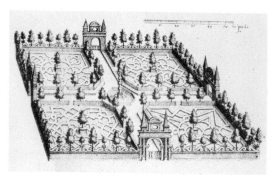

Fig. 27
Lawn with fountain, S. de Caus

Elizabeth Stuart

All this splendour was created by Frederick V not least for his wife Elizabeth, of the House of Stuart. Conscious of her rank and ambitions, she appears to have demanded such sumptuous trappings. Frederick, who seems to have loved her dearly, was at pains to fulfill her wishes to the utmost in the first years of his reign. But his unsuccessful plans as King of Bohemia also threw Elizabeth into the abyss. Fleeing through half of Europe, she found refuge in Rhenen, Holland, along with her husband. He she devoted herself to bringing up her children, but pecuniary problems and the meagre support on the part of her English relatives made her life difficult. A return to the Electoral Palatinate was out of the question for her, and her wish to spend the last years of her life in England was dashed by her sudden passing on February 23, 1662.

Fig. 28
Electoress Palatine Elizabeth,
Gerrit van Honthorst, c. 1620,
KMH, loaned by MWK

Fig. 29
Elector Palatine Charles
Ludwig, de Rüll, 1670
KMH, loaned by MWK

The Residence Deprived of Power

The Bohemian debacle and the outbreak of the
Thirty Years War (1618-1648), whose end Frederick
V of the Palatinate would not live to witness, affec-
ted the very core of the Electoral Palatinate. The
loss not only of the Upper Palatinate, but also of the
old Rhenish Electoral title, with the high imperial
responsibilities (arch-steward, imperial vicariate) it
entailed, were severe blows. The rivalry between
the two Wittelsbach dynasties had now been decided in favour of Elector Maximilian I of Bavaria
(1623-1651). In the Treaty of Westphalia of 1648 the
Electoral Palatinate was granted the Elector's title
anew, now the eighth, but it was now no longer
invested with the old privileges. Thus, the new
elector could not include the apple of the Empire in
his coat-of-arms.

Charles I Ludwig

In 1649, the successor and son of Frederick V,
Charles Ludwig of the Palatinate (1649–1680),
began his rule in Heidelberg. It was sad to see how
the land and the residence had suffered. The only
thing that could help was an immediate regenerati-

on of the affairs of state, the bolstering of the economy and the removal of the destruction. In order to regain the ability to pursue political action, not only needed the old ties with other lands to be cultivated, but also the standing of the new dynasty enhanced. With the rebuilding of the residential Castle the Elector Palatine attempted to give proof to his claim to power. Once again, it was intended that it become the midpoint of his regained realm. However, all he could afford were replenishments of ruined portions and decorations of the interior. Thus, for example, Ottheinrich Palace was given a new roof and the Hall-of-Mirrors Building a new interior. Charles Ludwig also began collecting art objects anew, as such collections had once decorated the Castle.

Despite this respite the terror of war was ever imminent, and renewed conflict loomed on the horizon. In 1672 King Louis XIV of France (1643–1715) began his expansion politics with a campaign against the Netherlands. In the process French troops also invaded the Electoral Palatinate and laid waste the enfeebled land. It was no help that Elector Palatine Charles Ludwig had given the hand of his daughter, Elizabeth Charlotte, known as Liselotte of the Palatinate, in marriage to the

Fig. 30
Liselotte of the Palatinate,
Hyacinth Rigaud

brother of the "Sun King" in 1671, thus entering into a direct relationship with France.

Fig. 31
Heidelberg Castle, from the north, Johann Ulrich Kraus, c. 1683, KMH

Charles II

In 1680 Charles I Ludwig died, and his son Charles II (1680–1685) came to power. The new Elector Palatine, of less than robust nature, became even more subject to the involved political quarrels of the states of Europe. France had occupied Lorraine and Alsace, and in the East, the Turks were on the advance against the Empire. The menace to the country from the West grew, and imperial assistance was not to be expected. The Elector Palatine recognised the danger and therefore had the defenses bolstered, which his grandfather Frederick V had neglected, and even expanded them. Beneath the fortress walls additional bastions were joined to the bell tower and the armory, such as the "Charles Entrenchment". By that, shelling from the other side of the Neckar would be less effective. But it was not only security that Charles II was concerned with, stately ostentation was also

Fig. 32
Elector Palatine Charles II,

Fig. 33
Castle courtyard, Johann
Ulrich Kraus, c. 1683, KMH

important. He had valuable furnishings made, thus adding to the Castle's beauty.

Now the entire complex had its old splendour. But his great problem was the unsettled hereditary succession of the ruling house of the Electoral Palatinate. For King Louis XIV was demanding considerable portions from the inheritance of his sister-in-law, Liselotte of the Palatinate, for his brother, Philip I of Orleans.

The Destruction of the Castle

Scarcely had the childless Charles II died in 1685 than Louis XIV marched his troops on the Electoral Palatinate. The Emperor's troops were deep in Hungary on the counterattack after the Turks' aborted siege of Vienna of 1683, so Louis realised that he had good chances of a military victory. The claim to the Electoral Palatinate, which he considered justified, was for him a welcome opportunity for settling things between France and the Hapsburgs once and for all. Louis XIV wanted to change the truce reached in Regensburg in 1684 with Emperor Leopold (1658–1705) into a final recognition of his reunificaton with Alsace and Lorraine. Moreover, there were more recent developments in

Fig. 34
Table with the coat-of-arms of
Charles II., Künzelsau 1684
Kunstgewerbemuseum
Koepenick

28

England which compelled the Catholic King James II (1685–1689), an ally of France, to flee. Louis' enemy, William of Orange (1689-1702), ascended the English throne, and the Sun King felt ever more encircled. Therefore, Louis XIV initiated hostilities at once with a manifesto stating his claims in 1688. Basing his case on an allodial clause in Liselotte's marriage contract, French troops occupied the Palatinate domains of Lautern, Simmern and the county of Sponheim. Then they advanced across the Rhine and conquered Heidelberg. At first the French commanders promised to spare the town and Castle, but the attack was a direct challenge to the German allies to counter it. In order to prevent the imperial troops from marching on the already gained provinces of Lorraine and Alsace, the French minister of war, François Louvois, decided on a "scorched earth" policy. An army of Lieutenant General Montclar, under the command of Peyssonnel, Mélac and Feuquièrs, was ordered to "plunder and raze" the land of the Upper Rhine, turning the land into a deserted "glacis". In order to render direct reinforcements more difficult, the systematic destruction of many towns, villages and hamlets was begun in 1688/89. Heidelberg, too,

Fig. 35
Ezechiel Dumas Mélac, 1698,
KMH

Fig. 36
King Louis XIV of France,
H. Rigaud, 1701

Fig. 37
Medal commemorating the destruction, J. Roussel, 1693

could not escape this fate, after Mélac ordered it burned on March 6, 1689.

The Castle was also attacked, and by setting fire to the roofs, the French explosives experts detonated the explosions they had planned. The Thick Tower and the Charles Entrenchment burst apart and fell down the hill. In contrast, the eastern and southern fortress towers withstood the attack. After the French had withdrawn, reconstruction of the fortress was begun immediately. But only the securing of the ruined buildings could be done at first. Thus, for example, Ottheinrich Palace was given a new roof, and the vaults in the Hall-of-Mirrors Building, Frederick Palace, the Apothecary Tower and the English Palace were shored up temporarily.

Meanwhile the imperial troops had consolidated their forces and begun their march on the French armies. Heidelberg was gradually given new defenses. But the entrenchments to protect the Castle from a new attack were inadequate. In 1693

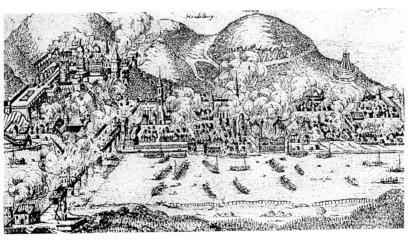

Fig. 38
Heidelberg in Flames, anonymous etching, 1689, KMH

the French advanced once again and had little trouble gaining control of the poorly guarded and scarcely armed complex. Now the work of destruction was to be finished once and for all. The old powder borings of 1689 were still there. 27,000 pounds of powder caused the towers and walls of the fortress to explode. The buildings burned down and were no longer inhabitable. The French writer Nicolas Boileau (1636-1711), who was in the army's ranks, suggested to Jean Baptiste Racine (1639–1699) that the announcement in the French

30

Academy of June 13, 1693 be as follows: "Je propose pour mot Heidelberga deleta, et nous verrons ce soir, si l'on acceptera" (As motto I suggest "Heidelberga deleta", and we shall see this evening if this is acceptable).

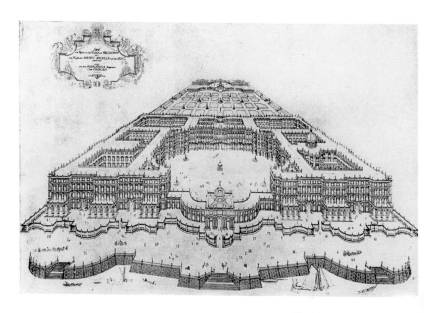

The Loss of Power

Fig. 39
Plan for a new residential palace near Heidelberg, Matteo Alberti, c. 1700, KMH

With the end of the middle Electoral line and after the destruction, power in Heidelberg Castle had been "extinguished". Now, in 1685, the Neuburg branch of the Palatinate Wittelsbachs, assumed the reign in the Palatinate in the person of Count Palatine Philip William (1685–1690). In Heidelberg he could not hold court. For this reason, the land was ruled from the inherited lands of Jülich-Berg, from the residence in Düsseldorf. The ruler, already an old man, died soon after, leaving the Elector title to his son John William (1690–1716). He took a greater interest in the Electoral Palatinate, as a small respite in the military conflicts had ensued after the Treaty of Rijswijk of 1697. In the Castle some renovation work was begun at this time, but for lack of funds a reconstruction was out of the question. First of all, Ottheinrich and Frederick Palaces were given new roofs. Then the Apothecary Tower and Kitchen Building were expanded to accommodate personnel.

In view of modern architectural developments, Elector Palatine John William was not enthralled with the old residence and even considered the idea of giving up the Castle in favour of a new Baroque palace situated before the gates of Heidelberg. In 1699 the Venetian Matteo Alberti planned a new residential palace in the style of the French Versailles on the shore of the Neckar to the west of Heidelberg. After this plan failed, a re-vamping of the ruined Castle was taken into consideration. Thus, a greater consistency of the courtyard façades was to be achieved and a Baroque modernisation to take place. However, the Elector Palatine was unable to have the two projects carried out, as construction under way in

Fig. 40
Elector Palatine Charles Philip, Johann Philipp van der Schlichten 1729, KMH
Photograph: KMH

Düsseldorf and Schwetzingen were such a financial burden.

In 1716, John William's brother and successor,

Charles Philip of the Palatinate (1716–1742), made the most of the opportunity to rebuild Heidelberg Castle after the end of the War of Spanish Succession (1701–1714). In so doing he provided for considerable alterations. According to his plans, the western buildings (Rupert Palace, Library and Ladies Buildings) were to be torn down, the moat filled in and the Artillery Garden lowered. A ramp from the west built up on arcades and of about one kilometer's length, which was designed by the Düsseldorf architect Domenico Martinelli (1650–1718), was conceived as a stately approach to the Castle. However, the Elector Palatine's efforts to re-catholicise Heidelberg and his plans to remodel the Castle had awakened violent resentment amongst the citizens of Heidelberg. The decision to reside once again in Heidelberg had been readily accepted, but the Church of the Holy Spirit was not to become the Catholic church of the Electoral Court, but should remain the centre of those of the Reformed faith. Charles Philip's decision came abrupty: on April 12, 1720 he decreed that Mannheim would be the new residence of the Electoral Palatinate. He demoted Heidelberg to an ordinary provincial town.

Heidelberg Castle also remained in its destroyed state under Elector Palatine Charles Theodore of Palatinate-Sulzbach (1742–1799). Only security measures were undertaken to prevent the ruins from further deteroriating. A special accomplishment of this last member of the Wittelsbachs to reign on the Rhine was the construction of the Great Barrel of 1750. In 1764 another mishap befell the Castle: a bolt of lightning destroyed the complex in its makeshift state of repair once again: Ottheinrich and Frederick Palaces and the Bell Tower burned out. This, the move by the Electors Palatine to Munich, to assume the throne inherited by the Wittelsbachs in 1778, and the transferral of the Electoral Palatinate to Charles Frederick of Baden (1738–1811) in 1803 put a temporary end to all considerations for a reconstruction of Heidelberg Castle.

Fig. 41
Charles Frederick of Baden,
Karlsruhe c. 1815, SSG

The Ruins of Romanticism

"Of the monuments of ancient times, the architectural works can most likely have a lasting influence on literature. For the stone witnesses of the past stand on the open road and can hardly escape the perspicacious and thoughtful observer. They are amongst the least inaccessible, the most monumental documents of history and therefore have the most immediate, powerful effect on man", wrote Fritz Sauer in 1910 while looking at the ruins of Heidelberg Castle. His words address another special feature of the Castle's history.

Fig. 42
Exploded Tower, drawing by
Goethe 1779, Staatliche
Kunstsammlungen, Weimar

Whereas destruction and reconstruction of the Castle were the visible factors of its development in the 17th and 18th centuries, in the 19th century it became the object of emotional affection through romantic transfiguration, making it one of the major German historical monuments. It was not its artistic form, but the literary description of its real state which gained the Castle its unusual fame. It was indeed only a ruin, but for that very reason it embodied grandeur and decline, blossoming and suffering, thus stirring human emotion. With this ambivalence at its core, the building complex developed from the close of the 18th century onwards an attraction which enthused many poets and artists. No less a figure than Johann Wolfgang Goethe, who sojourned in Heidelberg six times (1775–1815), was repeatedly delighted by the view of the ruin in 1814: "Rose and lilly in morning dew / Bloom in the garden nearby; / Behind them, in bushes and cosily, / The rock rises to its height; / And surrounded by high forests, / And crowned by a chivalrous castle, / The arch of the summit makes its way, / Until it is appeased with the valley", the poet wrote in his rooms in the palais of the brothers Boisserée below the Castle.

Fig. 43
Johann Wolfgang Goethe, engraving, 1777

Fig. 44
Heidelberg Castle, Johann Christian Xeller, enclosure in a letter by Marianne von Willemer to Goethe, 1825

At least two things can be made out in these verses of the great poet: the nostalgic enthusiam for the mighty monument and the place it has been given in a culture which emphasised sentiment. With it the idealisation of the Castle complex begins; indeed, the Castle becomes a sentimental subject of romantic poetry and prose. Apart from the rediscovery of its architectural and artistic importance, it becomes above all the vehicle of new aesthetic values. Overgrown by plants and embedded in the valley, it inspires the travelling cavaliers to capture the nature scenes from picturesque perspectives. Moods come to be which are expressed in outpourings of melancholy effusion, such as Friedrich von Matthisson's "Elegy in the Ruins of an Old Mountain Castle" (1786). The dreadfully beautiful is suggested by

Helmina von Chezy, and Friedrich Hölderlin leaves this lofty impression: "But massively down to the valley hangs the gigantic / Fate-versed fortress, torn to the ground / By the wind and weather; / But the eternal sun poured / Its rejuvenating light over the aging / Huge image, and around it living ivy / Sprang up, friendly forests / Rustled down over the fortress" (Hölderlin's ode "Heidelberg", 1804/5).

Ludwig Uhland and Nikolaus Lenau, Joseph von Eichendorff, Achim von Arnim and Clemens von Brentano express their moods: melancholy, dreamy, as if in a fairy tale.

Fig. 45
Count Graimberg, drawing by
Georg Philipp Schmitt,
1843, KMH

Another person who was apparently touched by the charm of the ruins was the French nobleman Charles conte de Graimberg, who became a great mentor of the fabulous place from 1810. Having left his ancestral lands to flee revolutionary upheaval, the Castle enthralled him, and he began to advocate its preservation. With a "collection of antiquities" pertaining to the history of the Castle and its inhabitants he promoted interest in the complex. It became a touristic sight, and under Grand Duke Leopold of Baden (1830-1852) Graimberg's commitment succeeded in counteracting the gradual deterioration of the ruins and a vandalism which until that time had yet to be checked.

Taking in the Castle as a real historical monument played hardly any role at all in the revelling in and absorption by sentiment. But because the romanticists no longer treated the ruins alone, but saw them in the historical context, a didactic interest in the Castle grew alongside the literary one. In a schoolmasterly tone, the destruction of the Castle by French troops was pointed out, stirring patriotic feelings at the time of the Wars of Liberation against Napoleon. Now the Castle was elevated to a national monument which had unjustly been made to suffer. "Why did your feet choose rubble of the proud fortress / Of German princes to stand on, judging genius? / Even as rubble it raises / Boldly its head up to the clouds!" writes a traveller as early as 1807. People longed for the old splendours and attributed more and more significance to the history of the Castle.

The Monument of Art History

Whereas poetic and nationalistic sentiments for Heidelberg Castle were developing, the need for investigating the monument as an architectural entity grew, as well. Already in the 17th century first descriptions had been written down, but it was not until the 19th century that these works were significant for the history of architecture. It was historical writing in the Palatinate which presented the architectural development in its main trends. But an understanding of the Castle from the standpoint of art history was still missing. The emerging scholarly methodology is the beginning of the arthistorical treatment of the Castle. Thus, for

Fig. 46
Description of the Complex of Heidelberg Castle, Johann Metzger, 1829

37

example, a "Guide for Strangers Through the Ruins of Heidelberg Castle" (Leger 1815) is published. The first lengthy description of the Castle complex is written by Johann Metzger in 1829. In it, architectural forms are identified and their qualities discussed. Architecture and sculpture are attributed to styles. The architectural work becomes a document.

Fig. 47
Grand Duke Frederick I of
Baden, Karl Friedrich Moest
1906, SSG

A Monument of Historic Preservation

With the art-historical study of Heidelberg Castle, which took place simultaneously with nationalisation, the idea of rebuilding the complex came up. It was proposed above all because of steps necessary for its repair and preservation, as a ruin would be difficult to secure. The impetus came from the Castle Association, founded in 1866, for co-ordinating all interests in its use. German architects and engineers joined the appeal for restoration and, after a precise inventory of the complex, recommended that the buildings be rebuilt. A national euphoria for Heidelberg Castle broke out in Germany, which not only included Grand Duke Frederick I of Baden (1856-1907), but also reached the House of the Kaiser in Berlin. The Castle was to become a monument of German history.

Fig. 48
Construction of Ottheinrich
Palace (from Koch and Seitz),
SSG

At the same time as the nationalistically motivated plans for reconstruction, the methods of restoration and completion customary in the 19th century became controversial. After much discussion, a panel of experts under the Karlsruhe Building Director Josef Durm recommended in 1891 to preserve the ruins and not to rebuild the Castle. But as its preservation was seen to be dependent on providing roofs for the buildings, a few members of the government of Baden and in particular experts they consulted, such as the architect Karl Schaefer, took the preservation steps to be restorative ones. Thus, between 1898 and 1903, the construction and completion of Frederick Palace was carried out. In 1901 Karl Schaefer also submitted plans for the Hall-of-Mirrors Building and Ottheinrich Palace. But with Ottheinrich Palace, the final restoration came to a halt because of the unsettled question of the form of the roof. A "restoration in the style", which would have completed buildings with analogous styles, was now completely out of the question for the architects and art historians wishing to preserve this monument. The majority voted to preserve the complex in the form it had been handed down in. Georg Dehio, one of the founding fathers of modern historical preservation, came up with this programmatic statement in 1900: "We want to seek our honour in passing the treasures of the past in as complete a form as possible on to the future and not imprint them with the stamp of some current interpretation or other, which is subject to error."

Fig. 49
Karl Schaefer, Leo Samberger, Munich, early 20th century

Fig. 50
Georg Dehio, etching by Max Lange

The Touristic Magnet

Heidelberg Castle is a tourist attraction in Germany today. Untold visitors from abroad come to see the Castle grounds, a prime example of a European cultural monument of historic times. Even American and Far Eastern tourist groups enjoy the Castle's uniqueness and the free view over the broad plain of the Rhine valley. Even 200 years ago, when it became customary to travel through Europe, the first tourists entered its walls. Even then the mighty complex was much admired. Soon Heidelberg occupied a permanent position in travel literature. Also, in the 1920's, the Castle Festival became a special attraction. Today we are inundated by art-historical and historical literature, books of photo-

Fig. 51
The Castle Courtyard in the
Summer

graphy and advertising brochures. Detailed guided
tours inform about the history of its architecture and
Heidelberg's Electors. The interior, particularly in
Frederick Palace, are done in period furnishing, a
reminder of the times when the Castle had significant art collections (Graimberg). With the opening
up of new and improvement of hitherto accessible
sections of the building, the Castle will offer more
intensive information options. Special tours concentrated on various aspects offer access to the
thematic variety of the complex.

The Tour

The customary tour of today, which was already worked out in the 1920's, is only in part oriented to the architectural development of Heidelberg Castle. For one thing, this is because the buildings were not built one onto the other successively, and also because some of the ruined buildings cannot be entered. However, all the important, accessible parts can be viewed and offer a nearly complete look at the complex.

Fig. 52
Bridge House

The Castle Courtyard

After entering the Castle grounds through the Gate House (1), past the Artillery Garden (2) with the Elizabeth Gate (3) and the Saddle Room (6), one arrives at the Bridge House with the stone bridge (7). After passing through it and the Gate Tower with the large clock (14), the quadrangular Castle courtyard opens up, with its magnificent façades. Visitors who are in a hurry probably head straight for the Great Terrace (22) to enjoy the view of the city of Heidelberg. But they miss the attractions of the interior of the Castle itself, which are shown in the guided tour of the Castle.

Rupert Palace

Amongst the oldest buildings is Rupert Palace (15), named for Rupert III of the Palatinate (1400–1410), the German King, whose coat-of-arms (imperial eagle with Palatinate lion and Bavarian lozenges) can be seen on the left of the façade. Under

Fig. 53
Rupert Palace with a Gothic bay window of the Library Building

Ludwig V (1508–1544) the building was expanded by a massive upper storey. A coat-of-arms tablet with an inscription, dated 1545, documents further work under Frederick II (1544–56). Above the Gothic entrance a keystone is placed showing two angels holding a rosary in which there is a pair of compasses. Only the ground floor of Rupert Palace imparts an idea of the former furnishing. The "Hall of Knights" and "Model Room" still have the low groined vaulting of the 15th century with the supportive middle pillars. The Frankfurt master builder and sculptor Madern Gertener appears to have been the artisan. The keystones of the Hall of Knights show the coats-of-arms of the houses of the Electoral Palatinate, of Scheyern/Wittelsbach, of England and the Burgraves of Nuremberg. The decorative panes of the Gothic windows, which are replicas today, but whose originals have been preserved, are Swiss work of the 17th century. The large ornate fireplace of 1546 in the Hall of Knights is probably from the upper storey and is richly decorated with ornamental figuration. Presumably this significant work of the German

Renaissance is by Conrad Forster (who was in Heidelberg between 1545–52).

Model Room: in this room the imperial wars in the Upper Rhine region between 1672–1715 and with them the destructive phases of Heidelberg Castle are the main focus.

Objects: a landscape model, showing the phases of the war; a model of the Castle made by Eck in 1932 showing it in its undestroyed state; a model of it in its destroyed state, Eck, 1932; a topographical model of southwest Germany, with the places destroyed by the war around 1700, 1997; a painting of Liselotte of the Palatinate, from the studio of H. Rigaud, 1713/14; a portrait of Louis XIV, presumably German, from the end of the 17th century; destroyed fragments of the furnishings and war implements from the Heidelberg ruins, 17th century.

Hall of Knights: in future the older history of the Electors of the Palatinate will be shown.

Fig. 54
Ornate fireplace of Frederick II, south German, 1546

Fig. 55
Model Room

Library Building with the "Stag Moat" and West Ward

After Rupert Palace one enters the built-over West Ward (13), which directs one's gaze to the prison tower (11), also called "Seldom Empty", and the western shield wall. The "Stag Moat" (9), which is drawn around the Castle, is very deep. On the far side is the steep wall of the Artillery Garden (2), which was built in 1528 at the behest of Ludwig V to increase security. Turning to the right, the way leads to the destroyed Library Building (16), which was also built by Ludwig V. In former times, the

Fig. 56
Ludwig XIV., late 17th. cent., SSG

Castle library ("Biblioteca palatina"), the archives, the treasury and mint were located here. Only the ground floor has covered rooms today. In the south room are the remains of a mural from the period of construction. Also, canvasses in lunette form depicting drinking scenes from the late 19th century decorate the upper portions of the walls. In the main storey was the library hall, with smaller storage rooms above. Traces of wall arches show that all the storeys were built with vaulted ceilings. This is in keeping with the building's function as a place for securing documents and art treasures.

Fig. 57
West Front with Library
Building

Fig. 58
Codex Manesse, "Grosser Heidelberger Liederhand-schrift" [manuscript anthology of medieval German poetry], 1st third, 14th century, University Library, Heidelberg

English Palace

The tour leads over the western shield wall past the Ladies Building (17) to the English Palace (19). One enters it through its built-up foundations, the North Wall with casemates. Subterranean walkways connect the towers and defensive walls for concealed troop movements. An outdoor stairway on the Thick Tower (20) leads to its first storey. Unfortunately, no evidence of the arrangement of the interior of the trapeze-shaped building has been preserved. That the building must have been magnificently furnished, is witnessed by remains of Renaissance stucco work on the window walls, in the sumptuous ornamentation (festoons, fruits, etc.) of mannerism.

Fig. 59
English Palace

Thick Tower

The English Palace is flanked by the exposed Thick Tower, the outermost bulwark to the northwest

Fig. 60
Thick Tower, from the south

(nearly 40 meters high and with walls 7 meters thick). Built under Ludwig V in 1533, its uppermost storey was remodeled by Frederick V in 1619 and given a dining and festive hall. In the festive hall theatre performances (Shakespeare) and concerts took place. On the outside are statues of the builders, Ludwig V and Friedrich V, by Sebastian Götz (the originals are in Rupert Palace).

Barrel Building

Crossing through the English Palace towards the east brings the visitor to the Barrel Building. Built under John Casimir from 1583-1592, with its Gothic

Fig. 61
Barrel Building, view from the Terrace

windows, it is one of the most unusual buildings in the Castle. The Barrel Building is located to the north of the Ladies Building and topped off by a small terrace. It served as a kind of balcony, with an excellent view of the Neckar valley.

Abb. 62
Barrel Building about 1904,
before being restored

Ladies Building

From the Barrel Building the visitor moves on to the Ladies Building, whose foundation walls are amongst the oldest portions of the Castle (13th century) and formerly, with its four storeys painted outside in a square-stone pattern (17th century), rounded off the northwest interior courtyard.

Fig. 63
Ladies Building

Fig. 64
King's Hall

Only the ground floor of the building has remained, in which the "King's Hall", the great festival hall of the Castle, is located. Its furnishing stems from the 1930's. The hall has a direct connection to the upper storey of the Barrel Building, which has a Gothic ribbed vault supported by a middle pillar. A pump was once connected with the Barrel Cellar, with which wine could be drawn directly. Today festivities are frequently held in "King's Hall".

The Soldiers Building

Through "King's Hall" the way leads back to the Castle courtyard and crosses it to reach the Soldiers Building (37). As the name implies, the building was used by the guards as living quarters and common rooms. The Soldiers Building is flanked by the Well House. The cosmographer and Heidelberg professor Sebastian Münster reports in about 1525/29 that its pillars stem from Charlemagne's castle at Ingelheim and are of Roman origin. Material testing

Fig. 65
The Soldiers Building

and comparison support this thesis, so it may be considered probable.

Economics Building

To the east of the Soldiers Building is the Eco
nomics Building (35), which was built under Ludwig
V with no particularly sumptuous furnishings. In its
western portion the remains of the old baking oven
can be seen. Also, the rooms of the slaughterhouse
can be imagined. Today the Castle restaurant is
located in the first storey. On the east side of the
Economics Building were the old grand kitchen, the
large new kitchen and pantry rooms. They were
badly damaged in the War of Palatinate Succession.

Fig. 66
Baking oven in the
Economics Building

Exploded Tower

By way of the Economics Building the visitor rea-
ches the Exploded Tower (36), also called the
Powder Tower, as gunpowder was stored here. Its
origins go back before Ludwig V in the 15th century
and indicate that it was the main tower of the first
fortress complex. It was not until Frederick IV that
an octagonal upper storey with a domed roof was
added. One third of the masonry shell was blown
off of it in the War of Palatinate Succession in 1693,
falling into the "Stag Moat" below. This broken-off
wall has always impressed visitors and inspired
poets and artists to philosophical musings and
artistic depiction. Goethe himself drew the ruin of

the tower and thus erected a monument to the romantic aspect of the complex.

Fig. 67
The Exploded Tower

Fig. 68
Ludwig Palace

Ludwig Palace

To the north of the Economics Building is Ludwig
Palace (32). On the foundation walls of an older building, but within the ward walls, Elector Ludwig V
had a simple, massive building constructed in 1524
which was later destroyed by war (1693) and fire
(1764). It appears to have been divided into two hal-
ves (north and south), and its entrance was via the
middle tower, which still stands today. It bears the
coat-of-arms of this ruler. The interior decoration is
completely lost.

Fig. 69
East Front with Apothecary Tower

Apothecary Tower

Behind Ludwig Palace is the Apothecary Tower (34), which derives its name from the Castle apothecary, which was later located here. It was likewise built in the 15th century as a bulwark and refurbished for residential purposes in the 17th century.

Fig. 70
Ottheinrich Palace

Ottheinrich Palace

Probably the best known building in Heidelberg
Castle is Ottheinrich Palace (31). Built between
1556 and 1559, but not completed, it is outstanding
for its richly figured programmatic façade. During
the architectural decoration, the principles of
ancient pillar arrangement were followed in a new
adaptation to present the ruler's claim to power
through the figures. The 16 statues of figures from
the Old Testament and ancient mythology were probably intended to express the antiquarian interests
and scholarship of Ottheinrich.
Ground floor (from left to right): Joshua, Samson,
Hercules, David;
2nd floor: Strength, Faith, Hope, Justice;
3rd floor: Saturn, Mars, Venus, Mercury, Diana; top
floor: Sol, Jupiter.

An interpretation of the programme was already
attempted by Karl Bernhard Stark in 1861: "On the
power of the personality, the heroism of the people,
princely power is securely based; it has its centre in
the practise of Christian virtues, united with
strength and justice, and finally stands under the
influence of higher powers, a heavenly guidance
revealed in the course of the stars." Today attempts
are being made to link these characteristics directly
to Ottheinrich's personality, the explanation being

Fig. 71
Saturn,
A. Colin, c. 1558

Fig. 72
Ottheinrich Palace,
viewed from the Hall-of-
Mirrors Building

that the virtues attributed to him through the figures visibly proclaim the justification for his reign and the benefit it brings to the land.

The original statues were replaced with replicas and are now in the covered ground floor of Ottheinrich

Fig. 73
The Imperial Hall in
Ottheinrich Palace

Palace. Here, in the "Imperial Hall", in the presence chamber, the drawing room and the parlour, are also magnificent door panels from the Renaissance period. The ropes of fruit, trophies, the foliage and ringed decoration, worked out in meticulous form, are the work of the Dutch sculptor Alexander Colin, of Mechelen (1526–1612).

Objects: in the hall a coat-of-arms relief with bust of Ottheinrich (original), probably by Alexander Colin, c. 1558; in the Imperial Hall the sculptures Faith, Strength, Venus, Justice, Hope, by Alexander Colin, c. 1558, Diana, anonymous sculptor; Jupiter, Mercury, Samson, Saturn, Mars, by Alexander Colin, c. 1558; Sol, after Colin; in the presence chamber David, by Alexander Colin, c. 1558.

Hall-of-Mirrors Building

To the north of Ottheinrich Palace is the Hall-of-Mirrors Building (23). It is oriented in an east-west direction. Only its cellar rooms are covered over; the upper floors have been open since being destroyed by war and fire. The building was given a façade in the "ancient style", i. e., with early Renaissance elements, which did not fail to have an effect on other German palaces built in the 16th century. Four arcade passageways placed before the building are subdivided by squat arches and pillars. As a whole the façade has a more Romanesque than Renaissance aspect, but in details of the chapters or round heraldic shields of the builders, the intention becomes clear. The

Fig. 74/75
Hall-of-Mirrors Building

interior of the building, too, which derives its name from a festive hall with Venetian mirrors on the walls, was clearly in the new style. Due to the destruction in the Thirty Years War and War of Palatinate Succession and the fire in the 18th century, the palatial building of 1549 lost its rich trappings. Via its arcades facing on the courtyard its entrance portion and Frederick Palace are accessible.

Bell Tower

The northeastern corner of the Castle complex is occupied by the Bell Tower, which derives its name from the fact that a bell was housed in it in the 16th century. The Bell Tower is adjacent to the Hall-of-Mirrors Building, and as the northeastern corner, it is one of the oldest portions of the Castle. Built at about the beginning of the 15th century, it was

Fig. 76
The Bell Tower viewed from the Hortus Palatinus

Fig. 77
Bell Tower

rebuilt several times later. Ludwig V had it reinforced, Frederick II added to its height and Frederick IV changed it into a lookout tower which could be seen from afar. By now the three-tiered tower has been hollowed out, and is off limits to the visitor.

Frederick Palace

Apart from Ottheinrich Palace, Frederick Palace, begun in 1601, is certainly one of the most striking buildings in the Castle. This is principally because it displays itself to the visitor in an undamaged state. Not just fragments of a wall, but a complete façade, a richly ornamented roof and intact interior are its strong points. But these features came to be just one hundred years ago, in the manner of historicism. The still extant sumptuous façade decorations of the early 17th century in classical architectural arrangement (Tuscan, Doric, Ionic and Corinthian pilasters) were utilised. But the figures, which are inside the Palace today, have been replaced by replicas. Their arrangement is based on a kind of ancestral gallery of the House of the Electoral Palatinate. Thus, the direct ancestors of the Elector from the House of Palatinate-Simmern take up

the lower level, that of the present. They are Frederick III, Ludwig VI and John Casimir (from left to right), preceded by Frederick IV. Above them follows the row of selected representatives of the first Wittelsbachs on the Rhine. With Rupert I, the founder of the University, Frederick I, the Victorious (in the Battle of Seckenheim), Frederick II, the Wise, and Ottheinrich, the last of the old Electoral line, the most significant personalities are chosen. That the House of Wittelsbach also possessed the highest rank in Europe, is documented by the depictions of its emperors and kings on the third

Fig. 78
Frederick Palace, courtyard façade

level, on the second of the upper storeys. Ludwig the Bavarian was Emperor and Rupert III King in the German Empire. Otto and Christopher were elected rulers in Hungary and Denmark, respectively. Above this row throne the "fathers" of the dynasty, Charlemagne, Otto of Wittelsbach, Ludwig I, the first Count Palatine on Rhine from the House of Wittelsbach, and Rudolph I, the founder of the dynasty on Upper Rhine. In their midst the Goddess of Justice arises, as legitimation of the hereditary title. On the dormers are the allegories of spring and summer. They are symbols of temporal duration, the cycle of birth and creation on earth. The scupltor Sebastian Götz, of Chur, Switzerland, together with the master builder Schoch, carried out the programme of figuration in three to four years. The sculptures have a massive effect, but are nonetheless of fine workmanship.

Fig. 79
Detail of the façade of
Frederick Palace

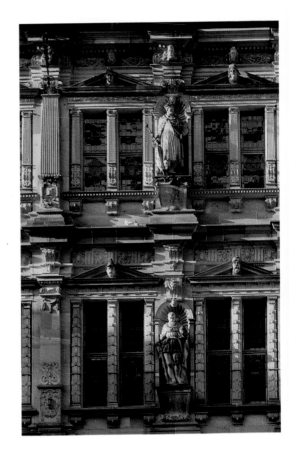

The Castle Museum in Frederick Palace

On the ground floor of Frederick Palace is the Castle Chapel, once consecrated to Saint Udalrich. Its foundations go back to the 14th century. As it was in danger of collapsing, it was torn down under Ludwig VI (1576-1583) and rebuilt. In the process, the main gate to the Castle, to the east of it, was removed. The chapel was built in the late-Gothic style, as witnessed today by the groined vault.

Objects: Charlemagne, Ludwig I, Rupert III, Rudolph I, John Casimir, Christopher, King Otto of Hungary, Otto of Wittelsbach, Emperor Ludwig the Bavarian, S. Götz, c. 1604/8; altar, 1st half, 18th century; organ, 18th century.

Fig. 80
Castle Chapel

Above the chapel, distributed over two main storeys, were the ceremonial rooms. In the uppermost storey were probably the servants' quarters. Hallways facing on the courtyard connected the four rooms to the north in the 1st and 2nd upper storeys, which faced on the Neckar. It was not so much the shelling in the Thirty Years War or the War of Palatinate Succession which caused damage

Fig. 81
Third room on first upper storey, photograph, c. 1904

to the interior, but the flames of 1693 and above all those of 1764. But the immediate construction of a makeshift roof prevented deterioration.

A complete restoration did not take place, however, until the late 19th century, when the Baden government commissioned the architect Karl Schaefer with a new refurbishing in the style of the Neorenaissance. Artists and craftsmen such as Karl Dauber or the Himmelheber brothers of Karlsruhe created richly ornamented rooms in the manner of historicism. The aim was thus not the restoration of former conditions, but an interior decoration which would harmonise with the exterior. But the rooms were never used as a residence of the rulers. In the 20th century museum inventory of the Heidelberg Civic Collections was stored here. The figures of the façade which had been replaced by replicas were displayed in the corridors. In the 1950's the Kurpfälzische Museum exhibited ancestral pictures of the Wittelsbachs, and the Badische Landesmuseum furniture, tapestries and art-craft works from the 17th and 18th centuries from their stored inventory, which, however, were gradually reclaimed by their original owners. A few years ago some precious items were again acquired for Frederick Palace. Some of them come from art dealers and some from former possessions of the Baden Crown in the New Palace in Baden-Baden.

Fig. 82
3rd room in 1st upper storey,
1996

On the first upper storey are art objects of the
17th and early 18th century, so as to impart an
impression of the whole range of forms of the
original, no longer extant, furnishings. These are
parts of the old loans from the Kurpfälzischen
Museum and the Badisches Landesmuseum.
Particular items, such as the magnificent cabinet
with verre églomisé, were acquired by the State
Palace Administration.

Objects
Corridor: limestone sculptures of Ludwig VI and
Frederick V, S. Götz, c. 1604/08. Room 1:
2 cabinets, south German, mid-17th century. Room
2: chest, Switzerland, 1649; chest, south German,
1st half, 17th century; table, south German, 17th
century; seating furniture, south German, 17th century; cabinet, Italy (?), 2nd quarter, 17th century;
portraits of Frederick II, anonymous, 18th century,
Elizabeth (Ludwig VI's wife), anonymous, 18th century, Ottheinrich, anonymous, 20th century. Room

Fig. 83
Cabinet with verre églomisé
paintings, Italy, c. 1680, SSG

Fig. 84
Moritz of the Palatinate
(1621–1652)
G. van Honthorst, 1640

3: cabinet, Italy, c. 1680; low cabinet, south
German, mid-17th century; cabinet, southwest
German, c. 1700; chest, Nuremberg, last third of
17th century; chairs, south German, 17th century;
Frederick V, Hendrik Goltzius (?), 1616; Elizabeth
Stuart, anonymous, 18th century; children of the
"Winter King": Moritz, Elizabeth, Henriette, G.
Honthorst, The Hague, 1640; Charles Ludwig, anonymous, 18th century; Rupert, anonymous, 18th
century; Sophie, anonymous, 18th century. Room 4:
cabinet, Upper Rhine, c. 1600; cabinet, Upper
Rhine, end of 17th century; chest, south German,
17th century; low cabinet, north German, c. 1700;
table, northwest German, c. 1700; seating furniture,
German, 17th century and Italian, c. 1600; Charles,
anonymous, 18th century, Liselotte, anonymous,
18th century.
The restoration of Frederick Palace was done in the
manner of historicism. But since the rooms of the
second upper storey were given almost no furniture
around 1900 and were later only furnished in a
makeshift way, the State Palaces Administration
decided to furnish them in a living style approxi-
mating the end of the 19th century. This also see-
med to be a good idea, as in no state-owned palace
of Baden were objects from the Bismarckian period

preserved. Due to the painful dissolution of the inventory of Baden-Baden Palace, items from the Neorenaissance period around 1860/1900 were acquired, as a reminder of the last great epoch of the Upper Rhenish monarchy. Heidelberg Castle was particularly as a domicile for a small portion of the formerly rich inventory of the ancestral palace of Baden.

Objects

Corridor: limestome scupltures of Rupert I, Frederick I, Frederick II, Ottheinrich, S. Götz, 1604/08. Room 1: chest bench, German, 2nd half, 19th century. Room 2: chest, Karlsruhe, 1881; grandfather's clock, Baden, end of 19th century; cabinet, Karlsruhe,3rd quarter, 19th century; low cabinet, Baden, late 19th century; refectory table, Baden/southwest German, c. 1885; chairs, Baden/ southwest German, 2nd half, 19th century; silver dish, Berlin, late 19th century; glass mug, German, late 19th century; wine goblet, Bohemia (?), late 19th century; lidded tankard, Bohemia (?), late 19th century; foot bath, Berlin (?), c. 1870. Room 3: low cabinet, A. Bilger, Karlsruhe, c. 1850; cabinet, J. L. Distelhorst, Karlsruhe, 1885 (design by H. Götz); small chest, Karlsruhe, late 19th century; refectory table, Baden, late 19th century; writing desk, Karlsruhe, end of 19th century; chairs, Karlsruhe, c. 1878/80; buffet, Karlsruhe, c. 1875; glass windows, H. Beiler, Heidelberg, 1886; bust of Grand Duke

Fig. 85
3rd room on 2nd upper storey

Fig. 86
Cabinet, Karlsruhe, 1885, SSG

Frederick I., Moest, taken from life, execution by
H. Klenze, Munich, 1906; flat-sided pitcher,
Mettlach, c. 1900; memorial goblet, J. Glatz,
Villingen, 1870; Ginori vases, Italy, 1870/80; wall
clock, Baden, c. 1850; chest for feathers, German,
end of 19th century. Room 4: buffet, Stuttgart (?),
c. 1880; low cabinets, German, c. 1860; chess
table, southwest German, 2nd half, 19th century;

Fig. 87
Heidelberg Castle, model by
Friedrich Freudenberger
Heidelberg, 1879

desk, German, late 19th century; seating furniture, Baden, c. 1860/70 and 1880; table clock, Baden, c. 1890; foot bath, German, c. 1870; tablet of tribute, N. Trübner, Heidelberg, 1906; majolica vase, Italy, c. 1870; model of Heidelberg, F. Freudenberger, Heidelberg, 1879; utensils, Baden, late 19th century; address by the Baden Association of Architects and Engineers on the 70th birthday of Grand Duke Frederick I, 1896 (GLA); carved wooden case of the Black Forest Association commemorating the 70th birthday of Grand Duke Frederick I, 1896 (GLA); address of a Munich citizen on the 79th birthday of Frederick I, 1905 (GLA); leather stationery folder, probably Berlin, late 19th century (GLA); desk pad, Baden, late 19th century (GLA); velvet

Fig. 88
Tablet in homage to Grand Duke Frederick I by the University of Heidelberg, SSG

purse, Baden, late 19th century (GLA); photograph stand, probably Baden, c. 1900 (GLA).

Speeches in Homage of the Grand Duke

During his long reign, from 1852 to 1907, Grand Duke Frederick I of Baden became one of the most popular German rulers in the Empire. His liberal policies were one of the reasons for this, but also his role in the establishment of the Empire in 1871,

Fig. 89
Address of Tribute Given by
the Heidelberg Students,
watercolour by Ludwig
Dittweiler, Karlsruhe, 1881

as he was a son-in-law of Kaiser Wilhelm I. The
speeches in homage from Baden – and throughout
the world – are thus representative of an unusually
broad public support of his reign. Festive highlights
in the relationship marked by mutual respect were
the ruler's jubilees before and after 1900. The
addresses in tribute given at the time turned out
more and more to be precious examples of handi-
craft art. As an appropriate ornamental style, the
self-assured bourgeoisie preferred above all forms
of the Renaissance, the "bourgeois" art. The quite
incomparable collection of some 800 addresses lay
completely forgotten after 1918 in Baden-Baden
Palace. In 1995 the Karlsruhe General State
Archives acquired nearly the entire collection and
has catalogued it.
In the General State Archives of Karlsruhe the full-
scale original designs by Carl Schäfer for the wall
decorations of Frederick Palace are preserved.
Schäfer also used Renaissance forms, in keeping
with the entire building. The rich ornamentation
was painted over in the 1970's, however, so that
here only a few selected work sketches in the
homage-address room bear witness to the former
wall decorations.

Objects:
Address of the Heidelberg student body on the 25th jubilee of Grand Duke Frederick I of Baden and on his silver wedding anniversary, Karlsruhe, 1881; address of the "Badenia" Club of Badeners in Nuremberg on the 70th birthday of Frederick I, Nürnberg, 1896; address of the Rhenish Credit Bank of Mannheim on the 70th birthday of Frederick I, Durlach, 1896; address of the Heidelberg student body on the 50th Jubilee of Frederick I, Heidelberg, 1902; address of the Badeners in Valdivia, Chile on the 80th birthday of Frederick I and his golden wedding anniversary, Heidelberg, 1906; correspondence folder, France, late 19th cen-

Fig. 90
Addresse by the Heidelberg student body
Heidelberg, 1902

tury; Carl Schäfer, designs for wall decorations in Frederick Palace, c. 1900.

The Great Barrel

A particular attraction in Heidelberg Castle is the Great Barrel in the Barrel Cellar. Under John Casimir, Frederick IV's guardian, the first such huge barrel was built by Michael Werner of Landau in 1591. This barrel had a capacity of 130,000 liters of wine.

Fig. 91
The Great Barrel of 1750

Elector Charles Ludwig had it replaced in 1664 by
Court Master of the Cellar Meyer with a larger one
(of approximately 200,000 liters), and finally, in
1750, Charles Theodore commissioned the cooper
Engler to make the barrel on display today (about
220,000 liters). Access to the Barrel Cellar is
watched over, as always, by the painted wooden
statue of the Electoral court jester, Clemens Perkeo
(documented between 1707 and 1728).

The Great Terrace

When the visitor ascends from the cellar floor of
the Barrel and Ladies Buildings and moves on into
the courtyard once more, turning left through the
passageway on the ground floor of Frederick Palace,

he soon finds himself on the Great Terrace (22) with the famed panorama of the city of Heidelberg, the Neckar and die Upper Rhenish plain. It was probably built by Frederick IV and covers over the old road up to the Castle with the former gateway building. From the Terrace the remaining walls of the Charles Entrenchment built in front of the Castle and the former Charles Tower (26) can be seen, built in 1683 under Elector Charles II. Adjacent to

Fig. 92
View from the Terrace of the City of Heidelberg

Fig. 93
Balustrade of the Great Terrace with bay window

the Terrace to the east is the former armory (25). Today it serves as a repository for stone material, as its roof was not rebuilt after the destruction.

Gate Tower

After touring the interior grounds of the Castle the outer portions should definitely be taken in. The

Fig. 94
Gate Tower

Castle courtyard is left through the Gate Tower to the south (14) and the Bridge House (7). Both are joined by a stone bridge, from which a good look at the deep outer moat can be had. After giving up the northern entrance, Ludwig V had the southern one built between 1530 and 1540. In former times, the coat-of-arms of the Electors Palatine was on the massive, high Gate Tower, held by two lions with two guards by their side. Both sculptures have been preserved. The bridge, originally a wooden

Fig. 95
Guards on the Gate Tower

drawbridge, was given a stone construction after the destruction of the 17th century.

Saddle Room and Elector's Well

From the Bridge House the way leads past the Saddle Room (6) and the Upper Elector'sWell (38) to the Hortus Palatinus.The Upper Elector's Well was rebuilt under Elector Charles Philip in 1738, so that fresh water could be drawn from it every day for his court in Mannheim. In the outer moat below this

Fig. 96
Elector's Well

well is the Lower Elector's Well (39) from the time of Charles Theodore (1767).

Hortus Palatinus

The tour of the Hortus Palatinus leads first to the large garden terrace in the middle, which permits an

Fig. 97
Hortus Palatinus today

Fig. 98/99
Father Rhine

unencumbered view of the lower terrace (57), the eastern fortifications (8, 29, 30) of the Castle, the supportive walls and Friesental. The once flourishing miraculous work is only revealed in its basic plan. Thus, the visitor can stroll through the Foliage Area (45), the Platform Gardens (46), the Seville Orange Grove (51), the Monthly Flower Garden (54) or the Maze (53). – But it is all covered by green lawns, from neglect and later alterations to the probably never fully completed work of art. And yet visitors reported in enthused tones about the garden. After all, in the 19th century the garden was used for planting rare forestry specimens such as evergreen oak, a cedar of Lebanon, giant firs or gingko trees. Goethe was inspired in 1815 by the garden, which was by then similar to English garden architecture, and wrote rapturous poems to Marianne von Willemer (1784–1860), which he published in his "West-Eastern Divan".

Parts of the original garden architecture are in the southeast corner of the grounds, the Water Platform with the sculpture of Father Rhine (47) and the Large Grotto (48).

Here is also where the narrow Upper Terrace (40) begins, which leads to the west and is complemented by a further, still higher level. This highest terrace also contains some parts of the first plan from the 16th century: the Bathing and Mechanical Instrument Grotto (43), the Grotto Gallery (42), the Palmaille Court (41), the Triumphal Gate of Frederick V (44), the former Venus Basin (50) and the Garden Cabinets with Elliptical Stairway (49).

Artillery Garden with Elizabeth Gate and Rondel

After descending to the middle terrace, a final short visit to the Artillery Garden (2) should not be forgotten, for from here the view to the west is most impressive. On the way there, one passes the Bridge House (7) and finds oneself facing Elizabeth Gate (5), a construction in the manner of a triumphal arch which was dedicated to Electress Elizabeth. The gate is the remains of a building constructed in 1615 strictly in the manner of the ancients and which served as a birdhouse. Some

Fig. 100
Elizabeth Gate with Artillery Garden

remains of the Artillery Garden walls and the blown-up Rondel (4) have been preserved. Through the gate at the Gate House (1), which was built in 1718 where the old, no longer extant "Fore-Castle" was built, the visitor takes his leave of Heidelberg Castle and takes the stairway down to the city or the cog-wheel train up to Königstuhl.

The German Apothecary Museum

In Heidelberg Castle there is not only a Castle Museum in Frederick Palace and the rooms for temporary exhibitions in Ottheinrich Palace, but also a separate and independent institution, the German Apothecary Museum. It was founded in 1937 and first opened in Munich. In 1944 it was bombed out, and after the Second World War its collections came to Heidelberg Castle via Bamberg. Here it was given a new domicile on the ground floor of Ottheinrich Palace. Apothecary paraphernalia and objects from four centuries, such as richly painted cabinets or faience receptacles, afford a very interesting look at European apothecary and medicinal practises from Gothic times to the 19th century. Particularly impressive is the medicinal collection with historic products from the mineral, vegetable and animal spheres. There is also an

Fig. 101
German Apothecary Museum,
Baroque apothecary from
Schwarzach, Baden, 1724

herbal room. Technical equipment, such as the "Döberein Lighter", probably the first of its kind anywhere, or distilling apparatuses in the Apothecary Tower round out the permanent exhibition.

Fig. 102
Apothecary paraphernalia from the Bamberg Court Apothecary

A Chronology of Castle History

1011
Emperor Henry II bestows Lobdengau on Bishop
Burkhard I of Worms.

9th to 12th cent.
Monasteries are established in the environs of
Heidelberg: the Monastery of St. Michael on
Heiligenberg ('Saints Mountain') in 863, that of
St. Stephen and Laurence, also on Heiligenberg, in
1094 and Neuburg Abbey in the Neckar valley in
1130; the Cistercian Monastery at Schönau in
Steinach Valley in 1142.

12th century
The bishop of Worms builds the first fortress in
Heidelberg, presumably on Small Gaisberg and
probably founds a small settlement in the valley.

1156
Conrad of Hohenstaufen, the half brother of
Emperor Frederick Barbarossa, becomes Count
Palatine and receives the Rhine-Frankish domains
as patrimony. He appears in the Heidelberg area
frequently.

1214
Ludwig I of Bavaria, of the House of Wittelsbach,
becomes Count Palatine on Rhine.

1225
Count Palatine Ludwig receives the Heidelberg
fortress as a fief from Bishop Henry of Worms.

1294
The Wittelsbach domains are divided between
Rudolph I, "the Stammerer", who receives the
Palatinate, and Ludwig the Bavarian, who is
awarded Upper Bavaria.

1303
Two fortresses in Heidelberg are mentioned in a
document: the upper fortress on Small Gaisberg
and a lower one on Jettenbühl.

1329
Treaty of Pavia: stipulation of borders; both
fortresses in Heidelberg are mentioned.

1356
The Golden Bull: Count Palatine Rupert I is confir-
med as Elector Palatine and invested with the
imperial titles of archsteward and supreme magi-
strate, as well as the imperial vicariate.

1386
Founding of the University of Heidelberg by
Rupert I.

1400
Rupert III becomes German King.

15th century
Expansion of the lower fortress to a representative
temporary residence; the inner and outer fortress
walls are built.

1st half, 15th cent.
Rupert Palace is built.

1462
Battle of Seckenheim: Frederick I defeats the
troops of Baden, Wurttemberg and the Bishof of
Metz.

2nd half, 15th cent.
Aggressive expansion of the Electoral Palatinate
under Frederick the Victorious and Philip the
Forthright.

1508–44
Under Ludwig V expansion of fortifications and the
interior Castle area: Ladies Building, Ludwig Palace,
Soldiers Building, Library Building.

1518
Martin Luther visits Heidelberg.

1537
The upper fortress is destroyed by lightning.

c. 1550
The Renaissance is introduced to Heidelberg
Castle: Hall-of-Mirrors Building.

1556–59
Elector Palatine Ottheinrich: the Reformation in
Heidelberg. Construction of Ottheinrich Palace.

1563

Under Frederick III conversion to Calvinism. The "Heidelberg Catechism" becomes the textbook of the Calvinist faithful.

1589–92

Construction of the north battery and the Great Barrel under John Casimir.

1601–10

Elector Palatine Frederick IV has Frederick Palace built and becomes the leader of the Protestant Union.

1609–14

Dispute over the succession to Jülich-Kleve. Palatinate-Neuburg is awarded the duchies of Jülich and Berg.

1610–20

Frederick V has the Hortus Palatinus and the English Palace built.

1620

After being elected King of Bohemia (1619) Elector Palatine Frederick V is defeated in the Battle on the White Mountain by imperial troops. Loss of the Electoral and royal titles. Expulsion from the Electoral Palatinate. Beginning of the Thirty Years War.

1622

Conquest of the Castle by the imperial field marshal Tilly.

1623

The Bibliotheca Palatina is carted off to Rome.

1648

In the Treaty of Westphalia Charles Ludwig is awarded the newly created eighth electoral title. Loss of the Upper Palatinate. Refurbishing work on the Castle is begun.

1688

The War of Palatinate Succession begins. In the name of his sister-in-law, Liselotte, Louis XIV of France issues the order to occupy the Palatinate and Heidelberg.

1693

Capitulation of the Castle troops, which is then pillaged and blown up.

1697

Peace of Rijswijk. After a short respite, Elector Palatine John William of the House of Palatinate-Neuburg, residing in Düsseldorf, has plans drawn up for tearing down the ruin and building a new palace on the plain near Heidelberg. All that results of this are shoring-up measures on Frederick Palace and the Hall-of-Mirrors Building.

1700–14

War of the Spanish Succession.

1716

Elector Palatine Charles Philip makes Heidelberg his residence and plans a rebuilding of the Castle.

1720

Because of a dispute between the Elector and the Protestant inhabitants over the use of the Church of the Holy Spirit in Heidelberg the residence is moved to Mannheim.

1751

The third Great Barrel is built under Elector Charles Theodore.

1764

Lightning destroys the Castle. Frederick Palace and the Ladies Building are given makeshift roofs.

1778

Elector Palatine Charles Theodore leaves the Palatinate to take possession of his Bavarian inheritance in Munich.

1779

Goethe visits Heidelberg Castle. The romantic transfiguration of the structure in literature and art begins.

1792

French revolutionary troops invade the Palatinate.

1799

Death of Elector Palatine Charles Theodore in Munich.

1803
Enactment of the Delegates of the Empire (Reichsdeputationshauptschluss): the Palatinate is dissolved, with its domains on the right bank of the Rhine falling to Baden.

1806
Charles Frederick of Baden becomes Grand Duke. Under his leadership increased protection for the Heidelberg ruins.

1810
The French Count Graimberg advocates preserving Heidelberg Castle. A collection of art works on the history of the Electoral Palatinate is begun.

1815
In Heidelberg the Russian Tsar, the Austrian Emperor and the King of Prussia conclude the "Holy Alliance" against Napoleon. On this occasion the Heidelberg ruin is illuminated by a great wood fire.

1st half, 19th century
Heidelberg Castle gradually becomes a national monument during the early period of tourism.

1868
The poet Wolfgang Müller, of Königswinter, propagates the rebuilding of Heidelberg Castle.

1883
Establishment of the Heidelberg Castle Construction Bureau, supervised by Building Director Dr. Josef Durm in Karlsruhe and directed by Regional Construction Inspector Julius Koch and architect Fritz Seitz. Work is begun to assess damage protection and future preservation of the ruin.

1891
Conference of a committee of experts from Germany on the rebuilding of the Castle. The decision is reached to preserve the Castle ruin as an historical monument; first attempts at formulating principles of preservation of historical monuments in modern times.

1897–1900
Restoration of the interior of Frederick Palace in the manner of historicism after designs by the Karlsruhe architect Karl Schäfer.

1913

Comprehensive art-historical description of the
Castle by Adolf von Oechelhaeuser in the publicati-
on series Art Monuments of the Grand Duchy of
Baden (vol. 8).

1954

The furnishing of Frederick Palace by the
Heidelberg Kurpfälzisches Museum and the
Badisches Landesmuseum in Karlsruhe with ancestral portraits, furniture and tapestries of the 17th
and 18th centuries.

1998

Furnishing of Frederick Palace with art objects from
the Baden ancestral palace in Baden-Baden.

Genealogical Table

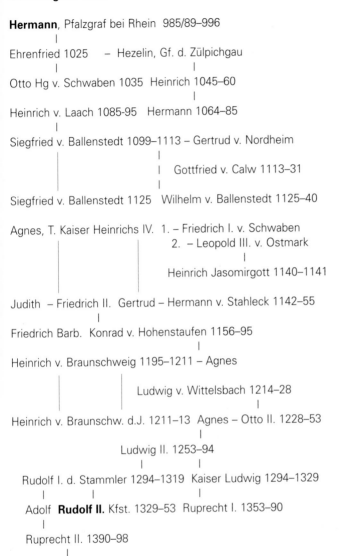

Hermann, Pfalzgraf bei Rhein 985/89–996
|
Ehrenfried 1025 – Hezelin, Gf. d. Zülpichgau
| |
Otto Hg v. Schwaben 1035 Heinrich 1045–60
|
Heinrich v. Laach 1085-95 Hermann 1064–85
|
Siegfried v. Ballenstedt 1099–1113 – Gertrud v. Nordheim
| |
| | Gottfried v. Calw 1113–31
| |
Siegfried v. Ballenstedt 1125 Wilhelm v. Ballenstedt 1125–40

Agnes, T. Kaiser Heinrichs IV. 1. – Friedrich I. v. Schwaben
| 2. – Leopold III. v. Ostmark
| |
| Heinrich Jasomirgott 1140–1141
|
Judith – Friedrich II. Gertrud – Hermann v. Stahleck 1142–55
|
Friedrich Barb. Konrad v. Hohenstaufen 1156–95
|
Heinrich v. Braunschweig 1195–1211 – Agnes

Ludwig v. Wittelsbach 1214–28
| |
Heinrich v. Braunschw. d.J. 1211–13 Agnes – Otto II. 1228–53
|
Ludwig II. 1253–94
| |
Rudolf I. d. Stammler 1294–1319 Kaiser Ludwig 1294–1329
| | |
Adolf **Rudolf II.** Kfst. 1329–53 Ruprecht I. 1353–90
|
Ruprecht II. 1390–98
|

Ruprecht III. 1398–1410 Kg. 1400–1410

Ludwig III. 1410-36 Stephan von Pfalz-Simmern 1410-59

Ludwig IV. 1436–49 Friedrich I. 1451–76 Friedrich Ludwig

Philipp d. Aufrichtige 1476–1508

Ludwig V. 1508–44 Ruprecht Friedrich II. 1544–56

Ottheinrich 1556–1559 Friedrich III. 1559–76 Wolfgang

Ludwig VI. 1576–83

Friedrich IV. 1583–1610

Friedrich V. 1610–23 Kg. von Böhmen 1619/20

Karl I. Ludwig 1649–80

Karl II. 1680–85

Wolfgang von Pfalz-Zweibrücken

Philipp Ludwig von Pfalz-Neuburg   Carl von Pfalz-Birkenfeld

Wolfgang Wilhelm August von Pfalz-Sulzbach

Philipp Wilhelm von Pfalz-Neuburg 1685–90

Johann Wilhelm 1690–1716 Carl Philipp 1716-42

Carl Theodor 1742-99 Kfst. v. Bayern 1778-99

Maximilian Josef 1799–1803 Kfst. v. Bayern 1799–1805
Kg. v. Bayern 1805–25

Glossar

Allegorie	Sinnbild
Antike	Griech./röm. Altertum
Architrav	Auf Stützen ruhendes Architekturstück
Arkade	Auf Stützen gestellter Bogen
Bastion	Vorspringende Verteidigungsmauer
Bergfried	Hoher starker Turm
Calvinismus	Dogmatische Lehre der Reformation
Dorische Ordnung	Älteste griech. Architekturordnung
Dynastie	Herrschergeschlecht
Erztruchsessenamt	Kaiserl. Hofamt
Fortifikation	Befestigung
Freitreppe	Nicht überdachte Außentreppe
Gesimsgurt	Waagerechtes Mauerprofil
Glacis	Leeres Feld
Gobelin	Wandteppich
Gotik	Kunststil 13.–15. Jh.
Groteske	Antike Verzierung
Halsgraben	Graben vor Ringmauer
Historismus	Kunststil 19. Jh.
Inthronisation	Feierliche Einsetzung
Jonische Ordnung	Griech. Architekturordnung der Jonier
Kabinettschrank	Aufbewahrungsmöbel
Kaiserpfalz	Kaiserl. Wohnanlage
Kapitell	Kopfstück einer Stütze
Katechismus	Christliches Lehrbuch
Kemenate	Beheizbares Wohngebäude für Frauen
Konservierung	Erhaltung des vorhandenen Zustandes
Korinthische Ordnung	Griech. Architekturordnung der Korinther

Krongut	Eigentum einer fürstlichen Herrschaft
Luthertum	Dt. Glaubensbewegung
Majolika	Keramikware
Manierismus	Spätphase des Renaissance
Mentor	Beförderer einer Sache
Mineur	Sprengmeister
Palas	Herrsch. Wohngebäude
Palmaillespiel	Schlagballspiel (pallamaglio)
Parterre	Erdgeschoß
Pilaster	Wandpfeiler
Pomeranzen	Apfelsinenartige Südfrüchte
Refektoriumstisch	Hallenmöbel
Reformation	Glaubensbewegung 16.Jh.
Reichsapfel	Kaiserl. Herrschaftszeichen
Reichsvikariat	Kaiserliche Stellvertreterschaft
Renaissance	Kunststil 15.–17. Jh.
Reunion	Wiedervereinigung
Ringelwerk	Verschnörkelte Verzierung
Romanik	Kunststil 11.–13. Jh.
Rondell	Turmartiger Vorsprung
Schildmauer	Hohe zum ansteigenden Hang gelegene Schutzmauer
Schisma	Kirchenspaltung 1378–1417
Schmalkaldischer Krieg	Krieg des Kaisers gegen reform. Fürsten 1546/47
Stukkatur	Gipsverzierung
Toskanische Ordnung	Architekturordnung der Römer
Trophäen	Siegeszeichen
Türnitz	Beheizbarer Hallenbau
Vorburg	Befest. Eingangsbereich einer Burg
Zwerchgiebel	Blendgiebel vor Dachgaube
Zwinger	Bereich zwischen Vor- und Hauptmauer

Literatur

Badische Heimat, vol. 43, 1963, no. 1/2, special
    issue on Heidelberg
Benz, Richard, Heidelberg, Schicksal und Geist,
    Sigmaringen, 1961 [monograph]
Bibliotheca Palatina, Eine Ausstellung der
    Universität Heidelberg mit der Bibliotheca
    Apostolica Vaticana, Heidelberg, 1986 [exhibition
    catalogue]
Debon, Günther, Goethes Begegnung mit Heide-
    lberg, Heidelberg, 1992 [Goethe in Heidelberg]
Dehio, Georg, Was wird aus dem Heidelberger
    Schloss werden?, Heidelberg, 1901 [pamphlet]
Dehio, Georg, Kunsthistorische Aufsätze, Munich,
    1914 [collection of essays]
Dehio, Georg, Handbuch der Deutschen
    Kunstdenkmäler, Baden-Württemberg I, (ed.
    Dagmar Zimdars), Munich, 1993 [art history]
Derwein, Herbert/Schaab, Meinrad, Geschichte der
    Stadt Heidelberg, in: Die Stadt und die
    Landkreise Heidelberg und Mannheim, vol. II,
    1968 [history of Heidelberg]
Fehrle-Burger, Lili, Die Welt der Oper in den
    Schloßgärten von Heidelberg und Schwetzingen,
    Karlsruhe, 1977 [opera in Heidelberg and
    Schwetzingen]
Grimm, Ulrike/Wiese, Wolfgang, Was bleibt.
    Markgrafenschätze aus vier Jahrhunderten,
    Stuttgart, 1996 [Margrave treasures]
Haas, Rudolf, Die Pfalz am Rhein, Mannheim, 1984
    [history of the Palatinate]
Heidelberg - Das Schloß/The Castle, Franz
    Schlechter/ Hanns Hubach/Volker Sellin,
    Heidelberg, 1995 [photo book]
Hepp, Frieder, Matthaeus Merian in Heidelberg,
    Ansichten einer Stadt, Heidelberg, 1993 [Merian
    in Heidelberg]
Kollnig, Karl, Die Kurfürsten von der Pfalz,
    Heidelberg, 1993 [history, Palatinate]
Kollnig, Karl, Wandlungen im Bevölkerungsbild des
    pfälzischen Oberrheingebietes, Heidelberg, 1952
    [history, Upper Rhine]
Levin, Herbert, Die Heidelberger Romantik,
    München, 1922 [literary history]

Manger, Klaus/Hofe, Gerhard vom, Heidelberg im poetischen Augenblick, Heidelberg, 1987 [literary history]

Merz, Ludwig, Die Residenzstadt Heidelberg, Heidelberg, 1986 [history]

Mittler, Elmar (ed.), Heidelberg, Geschichte und Gestalt, Heidelberg, 1996 [history]

Neumann, Karl, Schloß Heidelberg, Wiederherstellung, Berlin, 1903 [preservation]

Oechelhäuser, Adolf von, Das Heidelberger Schloß, 8th ed., Heidelberg, 1987 (ed. by Joachim Göricke) [detailed guide]

Oechelhäuser, Adolf von, "Heidelberg – Baugeschichte des Schlosses", Kunstdenkmäler des Großherzogtums Baden, vol. 8, Tübingen, 1913, pp. 363 ff. [architectural history]

Poensgen, Georg, Kunstschätze in Heidelberg, Aus dem Schloß, den Kirchen und Sammlungen der Stadt, Munich, 1967 [art history]

Die Renaissance im deutschen Südwesten zwischen Reformation und Dreißigjährigem Krieg, Eine Ausstellung des Landes Baden-Württemberg in Schloß Heidelberg, Karlsruhe, 1986 [exhibition catalogue]

Sauer, Fritz, Das Heidelberger Schloß im Spiegel der Literatur, Heidelberg, 1910 [literary history]

Schaab, Meinrad, Geschichte der Kurpfalz, vol. 1 & 2, Stuttgart, 1988; 1992

Strack, Friedrich (ed.), Heidelberg im säkularen Umbruch, Stuttgart 1987 [literary history]

Valentiner, Wilhelm R., Zur Geschichte des Streits um die Erhaltung des Ottheinrichsbaues auf dem Schloß Heidelberg, Heidelberg, 1903 [preservation

Vetter, Roland, Heidelberg Heidelberga deleata, Heidelbergs zweite Zerstörung im Orléanschen Krieg und die französische Kampagne von 1693, Heidelberg, 1989 [Castle destruction]

Walther, Gerhard, Der Heidelberger Schloßgarten, Heidelberg, 1990 [Castle Gardens]

Index of Names

Adolf von Nassau, Dt. König (um 1248–1298) 8
Alberti, Matteo (1646–1735) 31, 32
Antoni, Bildhauer 17
Arnim, Achim von (1781–1831) 36

Behaim, Bartel (1502–1540) 13
Beham, Sebald (1500–1550) 14
Beiler, Hermann 65
Bilger, Anton 65
Boiloeau-Despréaux, Nicolas (1636–1711) 30
Boisserée, Sulpiz (1783–1854) 35
Brentano, Clemens von (1778–1842) 36
Burkhard I. von Worms 78

Carl Philipp von Pfalz-Neuburg, Kurfürst (1661–1742)
    32, 33, 72, 81
Carl Theodor von Pfalz-Sulzbach, Kurfürst
    (1724–1799) 33, 69, 72, 81
Caus, Salomon de (1576–1626) 22, 23
Chezy, Helmina von (1783–1856) 35
Christoph III. von der Pfalz, König von Dänemark
    (1416–1448) 60, 61
Colin, Alexander (1526–1612) 17, 55, 56

Dauber, Karl 62
Dehio, Georg (1850–1932) 39
Distelhorst, Josef L. 65
Dittweiler, Ludwig (1844–1891) 68
Dorothea von Dänemark (1520–1580) 13
Durm, Josef (1837–1919) 39, 82

Eck 43
Elisabeth Stuart, Kurfürstin (1596–1662) 20, 24,
    64, 75
Elisabeth von der Pfalz, Kurfürstin (1539–1582) 63
Elisabeth von der Pfalz (1618–1680) 64
Eichendorff, Joseph Freiherr von (1788–1857) 36
Engler, Faßbauer 70

Ferdinand II., Kaiser (1578–1637) 20
Feuquières, Antoine 29
Forster, Conrad (um 1550) 43
Fouquières, Jacques (1580–1659) 22
Freudenberger, Friedrich 66, 67
Friedrich Barbarossa, Kaiser (1122–1190) 6, 78
Friedrich I., Großherzog von Baden (1826–1907) 38,
    65, 67, 68, 69

Friedrich I., Kurfürst von der Pfalz (1425–1476) 10,
    59, 79
Friedrich II., Kurfürst von der Pfalz (1482–1556)
    13, 14, 15, 42, 43, 58, 59, 63, 65
Friedrich III. von Pfalz-Simmern, Kurfürst
    (1515–1576) 17, 59, 80
Friedrich IV. von Pfalz-Simmern, Kurfürst
    (1574–1610) 17, 18, 19, 20, 50, 58, 59, 69, 80
Friedrich V. von Pfalz-Simmern, Kurfürst
    (1596–1632) 20, 21, 23, 24, 25, 47, 63, 64,
    75, 80

Gertener, Madern (1360–1430) 42
Gertrud von Schwaben (um 1104–1191) 6
Glatz, Johann 66
Goethe, Johann Wolfgang von (1749–1832) 34, 35,
    51
Goltzius, Hendrik (1558–1617) 64
Götz, Hermann (1848–1901) 65
Götz, Sebastian (1604–1621 nachweisbar) 12, 18,
    19, 47, 60, 61, 63, 65
Graimberg, Charles Graf von (1774–1864) 36, 82

Heinrich II., Dt. Kaiser (973–1024) 78
Heinrich von Worms 78
Henriette von der Pfalz-Simmern (1626–1651) 64
Himmelheber, Gebrüder 62
Hölderlin, Friedrich (1770–1843) 36
Honthorst, Gerrit van (1590–1656) 20, 24, 64

Jacob I., König von England (1566–1625) 20
Jacob II., König von England (1633–1701) 29
Johann Kasimir von Pfalz-Simmern (1543–1592)
    17, 18, 47, 59, 61, 69, 80
Johann Wilhelm von Pfalz-Neuburg, Kurfürst
    (1658–1716) 31, 32, 81
Jones, Inigo (1573–1652) 23

Karl der Große 49, 60, 61
Karl V., Kaiser (1500–1558) 13
Karl Friedrich Großherzog von Baden (1728–1811)
    33, 82
Karl I. Ludwig von Pfalz-Simmern, Kurfürst
    (1617–1680) 25, 27, 64, 69, 80
Karl II. von Pfalz-Simmern, Kurfürst (1651–1685)
    27, 28, 71
Klenze, H. 65

Koch, Julius (1852–1913) 8, 11, 38, 82
Koester, Christian Philipp (1784–1851) 21
Konrad von Hohenstaufen (1135–1195) 6, 78
Kraus, Johann Ulrich (1655–1719) 15, 27, 28

Lange, Max (*1868) 39
Leger, Thomas A. 38
Lenau, Nikolaus (1802–1850) 36
Leopold, Großherzog von Baden (1790–1852) 36
Leopold, Kaiser (1640–1705) 28
Liselotte von Pfalz-Simmern (1652–1722) 26, 27,
    28, 29, 43, 64, 80
Louvois, Francois Marquis de (1641–1691) 29
Ludwig von Bayern, Dt. König (1282–1347) 60, 61,
    78
Ludwig II., Herzog von Oberbayern (1229–1294) 8
Ludwig XIV., König von Frankreich (1638–1715)
    26, 28, 29, 37, 43, 80
Ludwig V., Kurfürst von der Pfalz (1478–1544)
    10, 11, 12, 13, 16, 27, 42, 44, 47, 50, 52, 58,
    72, 79
Ludwig VI. von Pfalz-Simmern, Kurfürst
    (1539–1583) 17, 59, 61, 63
Ludwig I. von Wittelsbach (1174–1231) 7, 60, 61,
    78
Luther, Martin (1483–1546) 12, 79

Martinelli, Domenico (1650–1718) 33
Matthisson, Friedrich von (1761–1831) 35
Maximilian, Kurfürst von Bayern (1573–1651) 25
Meyer, Hofkellermeister 69
Mélac, Ezéchiel Dumas († 1709) 29
Melanchton, Philipp (1497–1560) 17
Merian, Matthäus (1593–1650) 7
Metzger, Johann 37, 38
Moest, Friedrich (1838–1929) 65
Montclar, Joseph Baron de 29
Moritz von Pfalz-Simmern (1621–1654) 64
Müller, Wolfgang 82
Münster, Sebastian (1488–1552) 10, 49

Napoleon I., Kaiser von Frankreich (1769–1821) 82

Oechelhäuser, Adolf von (1852–1923) 83
Otto von Niederbayern, König von Ungarn
    (1261–1313) 60, 61
Otto von Wittelsbach (1206–1253) 60, 61

Ottheinrich, Kurfürst von der Pfalz (1502–1559)
13, 14, 15, 17, 59, 63, 65, 79

Palladio, Andrea (1508–1580) 23
Perkeo, Clemens, Pfälz. Hofnarr (1707–1728) 70
Peyssonnel 29
Philipp I. von Orléans (1640–1701) 28
Philipp, Kurfürst von der Pfalz (1448–1508) 12, 79
Philipp Wilhelm von Pfalz-Neuburg, Kurfürst
(1615–1690) 31

Racine, Jean Baptiste (um 1639–1699) 31
Rigaud, Hyacinth (1659–1743) 26, 29, 43
Roussel, F. 30
Rudolf I. von der Pfalz, Pfalzgraf (1274–1319)
8, 60, 61, 78
Rudolf II., Kurfürst von der Pfalz (1306–1353) 8
Rüll, Johann Baptiste de (1634–1685) 25
Ruprecht von der Pfalz-Simmern (1619–1682) 64
Ruprecht I., Kurfürst von der Pfalz (1309–1390)
8, 59, 65, 78, 79
Ruprecht III., Kurfürst von der Pfalz, Dt. König
(1352–1410) 8, 9, 10, 42, 60, 61, 79

Sattler, Hubert (1817–1904) 6
Sauer, Fritz 34
Schaefer, Karl (1844–1908) 39, 62, 68, 69, 82
Schirmer, Johann Wilhelm (1807–1863) 2
Schlichten, Johann Philipp van der (1681–1745) 32
Schmitt, Georg Philipp (1808–1873) 36
Schoch, Johannes (1550–1631) 19, 23, 60
Seitz, Fritz (1851–1929) 8, 11, 38, 82
Shakespeare, William (1564–1616) 47
Sophie von der Pfalz (1630–1714) 64
Stahleck, Hermann von, Pfalzgraf († 1156) 6
Stark, Karl Bernhard 54

Tilly, Johann von, Feldherr (1559–1632) 80
Trübner, Nikolaus 67

Uhland, Ludwig (1787–1862) 36

Virtruv, röm. Architekt 16

Wenzel von Böhmen, Dt. König (1361–1419) 10
Werner, Michael 69
Wilhelm I., Dt. Kaiser (1797–1888) 67

Wilhelm von Oranien, König von Großbritannien
    (1650–1702) 29
Willemer, Marianne von (1784–1860) 35, 74
Wolff d.J., Jakob (1571–1620) 23

Xeller, Johann Christian (1784–1872) 35

Heidelberg Castle
aerial photograph, 1993

1 Gate House with Castle entrance
2 Artillery Garden (West Wall) with Rondel
3 Elizabeth Gate
4 Bridge House
5 Caponniere (moat fortification)
6 Stag Moat
7 Prison tower ("Seldom Empty")
8 West ward
9 Gate Tower with Castle Clock
10 Rupert Palace
11 Library Building with Gothic bay window
12 Ladies Building (King's Hall)
13 Barrel Building with Great Barrel
14 North Wall and English Palace
15 Thick Tower with former Theatre
16 Frederick Palace with Castle Chapel
17 Great Terrace
18 Hall-of-Mirrors Building with arcades
19 Bell Tower
20 Former armory
21 Former Charles Entrenchment and Charles Tower
22 Great Battery
23 East ward
24 Protruding casemate (for covering the ascent)
25 Ottheinrich Palace with
   German Apothecary Museum
26 Ludwig Palace
27 Apothecary's Tower
28 Economy Building with Castle Kitchen
29 Powder Tower (Exploded Tower)
30 Soldiers Building with Well Hall
31 Upper Elector's Well
32 Lower Elector's Well
33 Upper terrace
34 Former bathing and music-box grotto
35 Former "Grotto Gallery"
36 Triumphal Gate of Frederick V
37 Former terraced gardens
38 Water terrace with "Father Rhine"
39 Great Grotto
40 Former garden cabinets and elliptical stairway
41 Goethe Bench
42 Scheffel Terrace
43 Lower terrace